QUILTS

From Tilda's Studio

QUILTS
From Tilda's Studio

DAVID & CHARLES

www.davidandcharles.com

CONTENTS

Introduction	6
Scrapflower Quilt	8
Scrapflower Pillows	16
Vintage Teapot Quilt	20
Birdhouse Quilt	30
Fan Flower Quilt	38
Four Block Quilt	46
Four Block Pillow	52
Cat and Bird Quilt	54
Cat and Bird Pillow	64
Cross Quilt	66
Plaid Quilt	72
Duck Quilt	78
Plum Party Quilt	86
Cosy Stripe Quilt	96
Cosy Stripe Pillow	100
Plum Garden Village Quilt	102
Plum Village Pillow	110
Plum Quilt	112
Happy Snowman Quilt	118
Happy Snowman Pillow	126
Materials	128
Basic Techniques	129
Patterns	133
Suppliers	142
Index	143

INTRODUCTION

Welcome to Tilda's studio, filled with quilts and pillows that you will love making for every season.

We begin in spring with the Scrapflower Quilt and its matching pillow, bright with flowers in pinks, yellows, teals and greens. The Birdhouse Quilt continues the garden theme with sweet little birds and their houses against a sky of fresh blues. The bolder colours of summer are excitingly displayed in the Fan Flower Quilt, with lilacs and corals glowing against a deep blue. For autumn we revel in the fruity colours of plums, peaches and blueberries in the Plum Quilt and the Plum Garden Village Quilt, with its cute houses and rows of fruit trees. Finally, we reach the cool greys and blues of winter with the fun Happy Snowman Quilt and its matching pillow.

On your journey through the seasons you will discover quilts and pillows suitable for a wide range of sewing abilities. You may prefer easy designs, such as the Four Block Quilt or Cosy Stripe Quilt. Or you might relish the challenge of the Cat and Bird Quilt and the Plum Party Quilt.

We have used fabrics from several of the Tilda collections. Specific details are given for those used, however, any of them can be replaced with others in similar colours. Many of the quilts and pillows can also be made in alternate colourways and a visit to www.tildasworld.com will show these alternatives. The projects have been lavishly custom quilted but it will be easy for you to use simple home quilting.

The instructions and illustrations are clear and comprehensive, so whatever project you choose to make is sure to be a success and add beauty to your home. I wish you joy in your quilting.

SCRAPFLOWER QUILT

This fresh and colourful quilt uses only one block but because it is made in twenty-four different colourways, it gives the quilt a charming scrappy look. There is also a version of the quilt with a sunny yellow background, which is made in exactly the same way (see www.tildasworld.com). A matching pillow has been designed for this quilt – see the next chapter.

MATERIALS

- Fabric 1: ⅛yd (15cm) – Peggy pink
- Fabric 2: ⅛yd (15cm) – Billy Jo red
- Fabric 3: ⅛yd (15cm) – Bonnie red
- Fabric 4: ⅛yd (15cm) – Nancy red
- Fabric 5: ⅛yd (15cm) – Shirly red
- Fabric 6: ⅛yd (15cm) – Billy Jo yellow
- Fabric 7: ⅛yd (15cm) – Sue mustard
- Fabric 8: ⅛yd (15cm) – Shirly dove white
- Fabric 9: ⅛yd (15cm) – Bonnie mustard
- Fabric 10: ⅛yd (15cm) – Nancy yellow
- Fabric 11: ⅛yd (15cm) – Shirly teal
- Fabric 12: ½yd (50cm) – Nancy teal
- Fabric 13: ⅛yd (15cm) – Peggy sage
- Fabric 14: ⅛yd (15cm) – Sue dove white
- Fabric 15: ⅛yd (15cm) – Bonnie sage
- Fabric 16: ⅛yd (15cm) – Peggy blue
- Fabric 17: ⅛yd (15cm) – Shirly blue
- Fabric 18: ⅛yd (15cm) – Billy Jo blue
- Fabric 19: ⅛yd (15cm) – Bonnie blue
- Fabric 20: ⅛yd (15cm) – Nancy blue
- Fabric 21: ⅛yd (15cm) – Pearls pink
- Fabric 22: ⅛yd (15cm) – Pearls yellow
- Fabric 23: ⅛yd (15cm) – Pearls teal
- Fabric 24: ⅛yd (15cm) – Pearls blue
- Fabric 25: ½yd (50cm) – Pearls green
- Fabric 26: ⅝yd (60cm) – Solid sky teal
- Fabric 27: 3¾yd (3.5m) – Solid cornflower blue
- Fabric 28: ¼yd (25cm) – Solid fern green
- Backing fabric 5yd (4.6m)
- Wadding (batting) 69in x 89in (175cm x 226cm)
- Binding fabric ⅝yd (60cm) – Pearls yellow
- Erasable marker

Finished Size 60in x 80in (152.4cm x 203.2cm)

Fig A Fabric swatches – if you can't source a fabric, replace with one in a similar colour

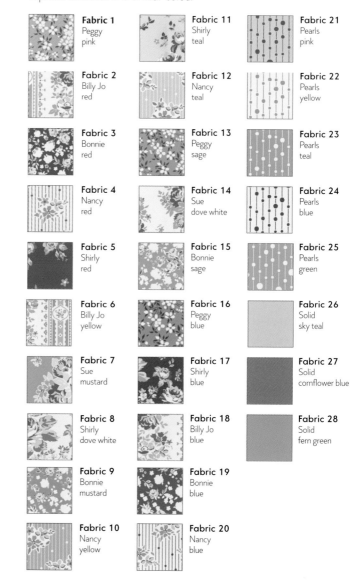

Fabric 1 — Peggy pink
Fabric 2 — Billy Jo red
Fabric 3 — Bonnie red
Fabric 4 — Nancy red
Fabric 5 — Shirly red
Fabric 6 — Billy Jo yellow
Fabric 7 — Sue mustard
Fabric 8 — Shirly dove white
Fabric 9 — Bonnie mustard
Fabric 10 — Nancy yellow
Fabric 11 — Shirly teal
Fabric 12 — Nancy teal
Fabric 13 — Peggy sage
Fabric 14 — Sue dove white
Fabric 15 — Bonnie sage
Fabric 16 — Peggy blue
Fabric 17 — Shirly blue
Fabric 18 — Billy Jo blue
Fabric 19 — Bonnie blue
Fabric 20 — Nancy blue
Fabric 21 — Pearls pink
Fabric 22 — Pearls yellow
Fabric 23 — Pearls teal
Fabric 24 — Pearls blue
Fabric 25 — Pearls green
Fabric 26 — Solid sky teal
Fabric 27 — Solid cornflower blue
Fabric 28 — Solid fern green

Fabric Note Where a long eighth or long quarter of a yard is given in the Materials list you could use fat eighths and fat quarters instead. A fat eighth is assumed to be approximately 10½in x 18in (26.7cm x 45.7cm) and a fat quarter approximately 21in x 18in (53.3cm x 45.7cm).

PREPARATION AND CUTTING OUT

1 Before you start, refer to Basic Techniques: Making Quilts and Pillows. This quilt is made up of a single flower block in twenty-four different colourways. There are forty-eight blocks in total, in a 6 x 8 layout. The fabrics used are shown in **Fig A**, the quilt layout in **Fig B** and the twenty-four block colourways in **Fig C**.

2 All of the blocks use the solid blue Fabric 27 as a background, so there are many pieces to cut. Cut these now, putting them in labelled piles. Their sizes are also given in **Fig D**. The shapes are squares and rectangles, so cut the fabric in strips across the width and then sub-cut into the sizes needed. The total numbers to cut for the *whole* quilt are given here.
• Piece **a** – 1½in x 4½in (3.8cm x 11.4cm). Cut 192.
• Piece **c** – 2½in x 3½in (6.4cm x 9cm). Cut 192

• Piece **d** – 1½in (3.8cm) square. Cut 384.
• Piece **e** – 3½in x 1½in (9cm x 3.8cm). Cut 192.
• Piece **g** – 1½in (3.8cm) square. Cut 384.

3 For the print fabrics, the exact measurements for cutting out the pieces for each block are given with **Fig D** – the print fabrics are pieces **b**, **f** and **h**.

4 Cut the backing fabric in half across the width. Sew the pieces together along the long side. Press the seam open and trim to a piece about 69in x 89in (175cm x 226cm).

5 From the binding fabric cut eight strips 2½in (6.4cm) x width of fabric. Sew together end to end and press the seams open. Press in half along the length, wrong sides together.

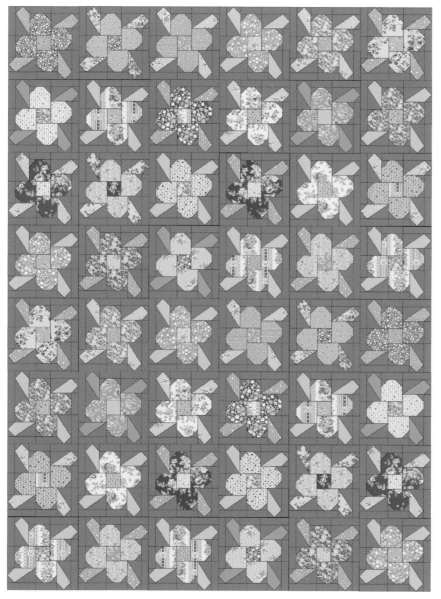

Fig B Quilt layout

MAKING A FLOWER BLOCK

6 A block is made up of four identically pieced sections (quadrants), plus one centre square. **Fig C** shows the different colourways for the blocks (Blocks A to X), so change fabrics depending on the colourway you are making. **Fig D** shows the layout of one quadrant of the block, with the letters indicating the cut sizes of the fabric pieces.

7 Cut out the pieces needed for the block (Block A is described and illustrated here). Follow the measurements on **Fig D**. Seam allowances are included. The Fabric 27 blue solid pieces have already been cut and for this fabric you will need to select the following for each block.

• Four **a** pieces.
• Four **c** pieces.
• Eight **d** pieces.
• Four **e** pieces.
• Eight **g** pieces.

For the Block A print fabrics, cut the following.
• Four **b** pieces (Fabric 25) 2½in x 4½in (6.4cm x 11.4cm).
• Four **f** pieces (Fabric 19) 3½in (9cm) square.
• One **h** piece (Fabric 21) 2½in (6.4cm) square.

Fig D Layout and cutting for one quadrant and the centre of a block

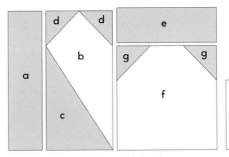

a 1½in x 4½in (3.8cm x 11.4cm).
b 2½in x 4½in (6.4cm x 11.4cm).
c 2½in x 3½in (6.4cm x 9cm).
d 1½in (3.8cm) square.
e 3½in x 1½in (9cm x 3.8cm).
f 3½in (9cm) square.
g 1½in (3.8cm) square.
h 2½in (6.4cm) square.

Fig C Block colourways
Numbers indicate fabrics used
Make 2 of each block

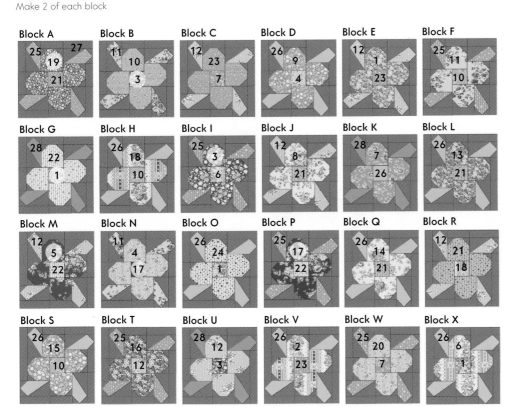

Block A · Block B · Block C · Block D · Block E · Block F
Block G · Block H · Block I · Block J · Block K · Block L
Block M · Block N · Block O · Block P · Block Q · Block R
Block S · Block T · Block U · Block V · Block W · Block X

Fig E Sewing pieces **a** and **c**

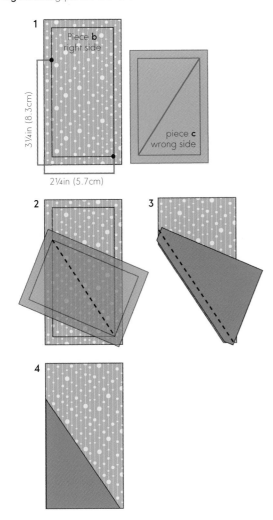

8 Make one block as follows (Block A is described). For the pieced section **b/c/d**, take a **b** piece and using an erasable marker, mark the ¼in (6mm) seam allowance on the *right* side of the fabric. Mark a dot at the bottom right-hand corner, on the seam allowance line. Mark another dot on the left-hand side 3¼in (8.3cm) up from the raw edge of the fabric, placing the dot on the seam allowance line (**Fig E 1**). Take a **c** piece of blue solid fabric and mark the ¼in (6mm) seam allowance on the *wrong* side of the fabric. Draw a diagonal line from corner to corner of the inner shape, in the direction shown in **Fig E 1**. Place the fabric pieces right sides together as in **Fig E 2**, carefully angling the blue rectangle so the ends of the diagonal line are matched with the dots marked on the fabric below. Pin in place and then sew along the marked diagonal line (you can sew past the ends of the line if you want). Trim excess fabric ¼in (6mm) away from the sewn line (**Fig E 3**). Remove the markings and then press the seam (**Fig E 4**). Check the unit is 2½in x 4½in (6.4cm x 11.4cm).

9 Add the corner triangles to this unit as follows. Place a **d** 1½in (3.8cm) square right sides together with the **b/c** unit, aligning the edges as in **Fig F 1**. Sew along the diagonal as shown. Trim excess fabric ¼in (6mm) away from the sewn line (**Fig F 2**). Press the corner triangle outwards. Repeat this process with another **d** square on the other side of the unit (**Fig F 3**).

10 Make unit **f/g** using one print **f** square and two smaller **g** blue squares. Follow the same process as above to create corner triangles on the print square, following **Fig G**. Check the unit is 3½in (9cm) square.

Fig F Adding pieces **d** to **b/c**

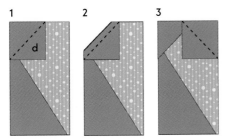

Fig G Sewing pieces **g** to **f**

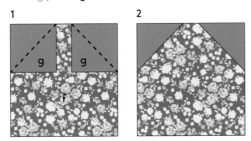

11 Assemble one quadrant following **Fig H 1**. Sew piece **a** to unit **b/c/d**. Sew a piece **e** to unit **f/g**. Now sew the units together (**Fig H2**). Make four quadrants like this for a block.

12 To assemble a block, lay out four quadrants and one centre square **h**, as in **Fig I**. The units need to be sewn to the centre square starting with a *partial* seam. Place the centre square right sides together with a quadrant as shown in **Fig J 1**. Sew the ¼in (6mm) seam but stop about 1in (2.5cm) away from the end of the square. Press the seam. Take the next quadrant and sew it to the block, this time sewing the *full* seam (**Fig J 2**). Press the seam. Add the third quadrant (**Fig J 3**) and the fourth quadrant in the same way, sewing full seams (**Fig J 4**). Finally, go back to the partial seam and finish sewing it, all the way to the end of the first quadrant (**Fig J 5**). Press the final seam. Check the block is 10½in (26.7cm) square.

13 Make the other block colourways using the same process and referring to **Fig C** for the fabrics to use for each colourway. Make two of each of the blocks.

ASSEMBLING THE QUILT

14 Follow **Fig B** carefully, laying out the blocks as shown. Note that the bottom half of the quilt has the same order of blocks as the top half, but reversing the block order in each row. **Fig C** shows the Block A to Block X order of the top half of the quilt. Sew the blocks together into rows using ¼in (6mm) seams. Press the seams of alternate rows in opposite directions. Now sew the rows together and press the long seams.

QUILTING AND FINISHING

15 Make a quilt sandwich of the backing fabric, wadding (batting) and quilt. Quilt as desired. Square up the quilt, trimming excess wadding and backing.

16 Use the prepared double-fold binding strip to bind your quilt (see Basic Techniques: Binding). Add a label and your quilt is finished.

Fig H Assembling a quadrant

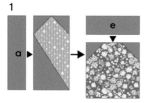
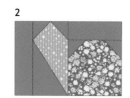

Fig J Assembling the block

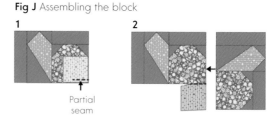
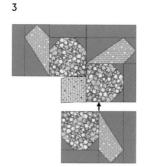
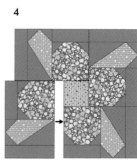

Fig I Laying out the block units

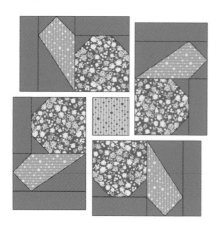

SCRAPFLOWER PILLOWS

These pretty pillows are wonderful companions to the Scrapflower Quilts. They feature four flower blocks in different colourways, framed by a simple border. The pillows use some of the same fabrics as the quilt and in smaller quantities. Refer to the fabric swatches in **Fig A** of the quilt instructions. The blue pillow is described. The yellow pillow is made in the same way as the blue, but uses Solid pale yellow in place of Solid cornflower blue.

MATERIALS

- Fabric 3: 12in (30.5cm) square – Bonnie red
- Fabric 5: 10in (25.4cm) square – Shirly red
- Fabric 8: 10in (25.4cm) square – Shirly dove white
- Fabric 10: 10in (25.4cm) square – Nancy yellow
- Fabric 11: 10in (25.4cm) square – Shirly teal
- Fabric 12: 10in (25.4cm) square – Nancy teal
- Fabric 21: 5in (12.7cm) square – Pearls pink
- Fabric 22: 5in (12.7cm) square – Pearls yellow
- Fabric 25: 10in (25.4cm) square – Pearls green
- Fabric 26: 10in (25.4cm) square – Solid sky teal
- Fabric 27: ½yd (50cm) – Solid cornflower blue (or Solid pale yellow)
- Wadding (batting) 24in (61cm) square
- Lining fabric 24in (61cm) square (optional)
- Fabric for back of pillow, two pieces 15in x 22½in (38cm x 57.2cm)
- Binding fabric ¼yd (25cm) – Pearls yellow
- Erasable marker
- Pillow pad to fit cover

Finished Size 22in x 22in (56cm x 56cm)

PREPARATION AND CUTTING OUT

1 From Fabric 27 cornflower blue (or pale yellow) cut the following for the blocks.
- Piece **a** – 1½in x 4½in (3.8cm x 11.4cm). Cut 16 in total.
- Piece **c** – 2½in x 3½in (6.4cm x 9cm). Cut 16 in total.
- Piece **d** – 1½in (3.8cm) square. Cut 32 in total.
- Piece **e** – 3½in x 1½in (9cm x 3.8cm). Cut 16 in total.
- Piece **g** – 1½in (3.8cm) square. Cut 32 in total.

2 From Fabric 27 cornflower blue (or pale yellow) for the outer border cut two strips 1½in x 20½in (3.8cm x 52cm) and two strips 1½in x 22½in (3.8cm x 57.2cm).

3 For the print fabrics, follow **Fig A** and **Fig B** here for block layout and colourways.
- Cut **b** pieces 2½in x 4½in (6.4cm x 11.4cm).
- Cut **f** pieces 3½in (9cm) square.
- Cut **h** pieces 2½in (6.4cm) square.

Fig A Layout and cutting for one quadrant and the centre of a block

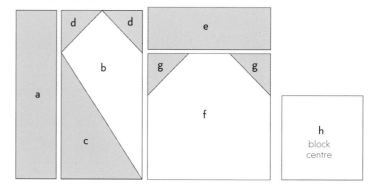

a 1½in x 4½in (3.8cm x 11.4cm).
b 2½in x 4½in (6.4cm x 11.4cm).
c 2½in x 3½in (6.4cm x 9cm).
d 1½in (3.8cm) square.
e 3½in x 1½in (9cm x 3.8cm).
f 3½in (9cm) square.
g 1½in (3.8cm) square.
h 2½in (6.4cm) square.

4 From the binding fabric cut three 2½in (6.4cm) x width of fabric strips. Sew together into one long length, press seams open and prepare as a double-fold binding.

MAKING THE PATCHWORK

5 To make the blocks follow the Scrapflower Quilt instructions (Steps 6 to 12). Make one of each block.

6 Once made, sew the blocks together into pairs and press. Now sew the pairs together, as shown in **Fig C** here. Sew the short border strips to the top and bottom of the patchwork and press. Sew the longer strips to the sides and press.

QUILTING AND MAKING UP

7 Make a quilt sandwich of the patchwork, wadding (batting) and lining fabric (if using). Quilt as desired. Trim excess wadding and lining to match the patchwork size.

8 Make up and bind the pillow cover following the method given in Basic Techniques: Bound-Edge Pillow Cover. Press the cover and insert a pillow pad to finish.

Fig B Flower block colourways
Numbers indicate fabrics used. Make 1 of each block

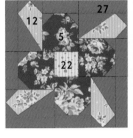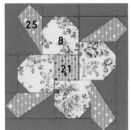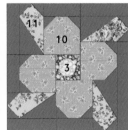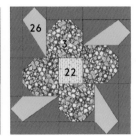

Fig C Assembling the pillow

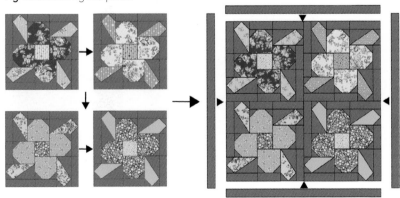

VINTAGE TEAPOT QUILT

This is the perfect quilt to have on display when friends drop by for a cup of tea. Three different teapot blocks in pretty prints sit on bunting-edged shelves. A fresh solid fabric is used for the background and this sky teal colour contrasts beautifully with the pictorial blocks. There's also a pretty fern green version of this quilt, which you can find at www.tildasworld.com.

MATERIALS

- Fabric 1: ½yd (50cm) – Bonnie red
- Fabric 2: ½yd (50cm) – Nancy red
- Fabric 3: ½yd (50cm) – Billy Jo red
- Fabric 4: ⅜yd (40cm) – Shirley teal
- Fabric 5: ⅜yd (40cm) – Shirly dove white
- Fabric 6: ⅜yd (40cm) – Medium Dots red
- Fabric 7: ⅜yd (40cm) – Shirly red
- Fabric 8: ⅜yd (40cm) – Nancy teal
- Fabric 9: ⅛yd (15cm) – Pen Stripe light blue
- Fabric 10: ¼yd (25cm) – Tiny Star light blue
- Fabric 11: ⅜yd (40cm) – Crisscross light blue
- Fabric 12: ¼yd (25cm) – Paint Dots light blue
- Fabric 13: ¼yd (25cm) – Tiny Dots light blue
- Fabric 14: ⅛yd (15cm) – Dottie Dots light blue
- Fabric 15: 3⅜yd (3m) – Solid sky teal
- Backing fabric 3½yd (3.2m)
- Wadding (batting) 60in x 82in (152.4cm x 208.3cm)
- Binding fabric ½yd (50cm) – Pearls yellow
- Removable fabric marker

Finished Size 52in x 74in (132cm x 188cm)

Fabric Note Where a long eighth or long quarter of a yard is given in the Materials list you could use fat eighths and fat quarters instead. A fat eighth is assumed to be approx. 10½in x 18in (26.7cm x 45.7cm) and a fat quarter approx. 21in x 18in (53.3cm x 45.7cm).

Fig A Fabric swatches – if you can't source a fabric, replace with one in a similar colour

Fabric 1
Bonnie
red

Fabric 9
Pen Stripe
light blue

Fabric 2
Nancy
red

Fabric 10
Tiny Star
light blue

Fabric 3
Billy Jo
red

Fabric 11
Crisscross
light blue

Fabric 4
Shirly
teal

Fabric 12
Paint Dots
light blue

Fabric 5
Shirly
dove white

Fabric 13
Tiny Dots
light blue

Fabric 6
Medium Dots
red

Fabric 14
Dottie Dots
light blue

Fabric 7
Shirly
red

Fabric 15
Solid
sky teal

Fabric 8
Nancy
teal

PREPARATION AND CUTTING OUT

1 Before you start, refer to Basic Techniques: Making Quilts and Pillows. This quilt is made up of three different teapot blocks – Block 1 (in two different colourways), Block 2 (in four different colourways) and Block 3 (in two different colourways). The teapots are arranged in rows, separated by narrow sashing strips. Narrow rows of flying geese blocks are used like bunting between the teapot rows. The fabrics used are shown in **Fig A** and the quilt layout in **Fig B**. The different colourways for the teapot blocks are shown in **Fig C**.

2 For the print fabrics for the teapot blocks, follow the exact measurements for cutting out the pieces for each block in **Fig D**, **Fig E** and **Fig F**. Seam allowances are included in these measurements.

Fig B Quilt layout

3 All of the teapot blocks use the solid sky teal Fabric 15 as a background, so there are many pieces to cut. You could cut these now if desired, putting them in labelled piles (or cut the pieces as you make each block). Use the cut sizes given in **Fig D**, **Fig E** and **Fig F**. The shapes are squares and rectangles, so cut the fabric in strips across the width and then sub-cut into the sizes needed.

4 For the Fabric 15 vertical sashing strips cut thirty 1¼in x 10½in (3.2cm x 26.7cm).

5 For the flying geese blocks cut 182 squares 2½in (6.4cm) from Fabric 15.

6 For the flying geese blocks cut 4½in x 2½in (11.4cm x 6.4cm) rectangles (ninety-one in total) from the following print fabrics.
- Fabric 1 – sixteen rectangles.
- Fabric 2 – twelve rectangles.
- Fabric 3 – twelve rectangles.
- Fabric 4 – twelve rectangles.
- Fabric 5 – twelve rectangles.
- Fabric 6 – nine rectangles.
- Fabric 7 – nine rectangles.
- Fabric 8 – nine rectangles.

Fig C Block colourways
Numbers indicate fabrics (see Fig A)
Make 3 of each block

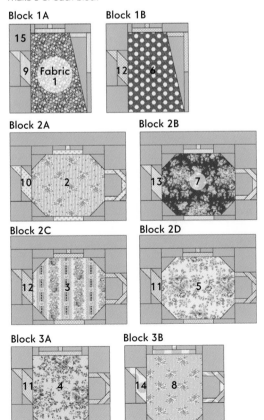

Block 1A Block 1B
Block 2A Block 2B
Block 2C Block 2D
Block 3A Block 3B

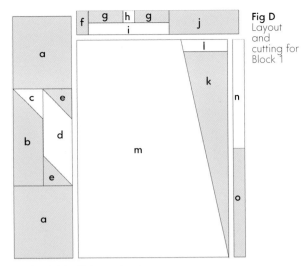

Fig D
Layout and cutting for Block 1

a 3in x 3½in (7.6cm x 9cm).
b 1¾in x 4½in (4.4cm x 11.4cm).
c 1¾in (4.4cm) square.
d 1¾in x 4½in (4.4cm x 11.4cm).
e 1¾in (4.4cm) square.
f 1in x 1½in (2.5cm x 3.8cm).
g 2in x 1in (5.1cm x 2.5cm).
h 1in (2.5cm) square.
i 4in x 1in (10.2cm x 2.5cm).
j 3½in x 1½in (9cm x 3.8cm).
k 2½in x 9in (6.4cm x 23cm).
l 2½in x 1in (6.4cm x 2.5cm).
m 7in x 9½in (17.8cm x 24.1cm).
n 1in x 5in (2.5cm x 12.7cm).
o 1in x 5in (2.5cm x 12.7cm).

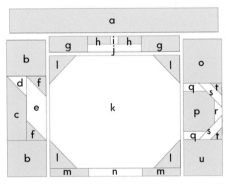

Fig E Layout and cutting for Block 2

a 14in x 2in (35.5cm x 5.1cm).
b 3in x 2¾in (7.6cm x 7cm).
c 1¾in x 4½in (4.4cm x 11.4cm).
d 1¾in (4.4cm) square.
e 1¾in x 4½in (4.4cm x 11.4cm).
f 1¾in (4.4cm) square.
g 3in x 1½in (7.6cm x 3.8cm).
h 2in x 1in (5.1cm x 2.5cm).
i 1in (2.5cm) square.
j 4in x 1in (10.2cm x 2.5cm).
k 9in x 7½in (23cm x 19cm).
l 2¼in (5.7cm) square.
m 3in x 1in (7.6cm x 2.5cm).
n 4in x 1in (10.2cm x 2.5cm).
o 3in x 3¼in (7.6cm x 8.3cm).
p 2½in x 3in (6.4cm x 7.6cm).
q 2½in x 1in (6.4cm x 2.5cm).
r 1in x 4in (2.5cm x 10.2cm).
s 2in (5.1cm) square.
t 1¼in (3.2cm) square.
u 3in x 2¾in (7.6cm x 7cm).

Fig F Layout and cutting for Block 3

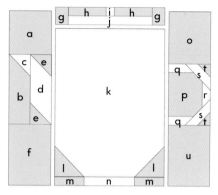

a 3in (7.6cm) square.
b 1¾in x 4½in (4.4cm x 11.4cm).
c 1¾in (4.4cm) square.
d 1¾in x 4½in (4.4cm x 11.4cm).
e 1¾in (4.4cm) square.
f 3in x 4in (7.6cm x 10.2cm).
g 1¼in x 1½in (3.2cm x 3.8cm).
h 2¾in x 1in (7cm x 2.5cm).
i 1in (2.5cm) square.
j 5½in x 1in (14cm x 2.5cm).
k 7in x 9in (17.8cm x 23cm).
l 2¼in (5.7cm) square.
m 2¼in x 1in (5.7cm x 2.5cm).
n 3½in x 1in (9cm x 2.5cm).
o 3in x 3½in (7.6cm x 9cm).
p 2½in x 3in (6.4cm x 7.6cm).
q 2½in x 1in (6.4cm x 2.5cm).
r 1in x 4in (2.5cm x 10.2cm).
s 2in (5.1cm) square.
t 1¼in (3.2cm) square.
u 3in x 4in (7.6cm x 10.2cm).

7 Cut the backing fabric in half across the width. Sew together along the long side. Press the seam open and trim to a piece about 60in x 82in (152.4cm x 208.3cm).

8 From the binding fabric cut seven strips 2½in (6.4cm) x width of fabric. Sew together end to end and press seams open. Press in half along the length, wrong sides together.

MAKING A BLOCK 1 TEAPOT

9 Each Block 1 is made the same way, but in two different colourways (see **Fig C**). Block 1A is described in detail here. **Fig D** shows the layout of the block, with the letters indicating the cut sizes of the fabric pieces. When you have cut all the pieces for one block, lay them out in the different sections of the block as best you can.

10 Follow **Fig G** for sewing the spout. Create a triangle on a corner as follows. On the wrong side of a **c** square mark a diagonal line. Place the square right sides together with piece **b**, matching the top edges. Sew along the marked diagonal. Trim excess fabric ¼in (6mm) away from the sewn line and press the corner outwards. Repeat this process with piece **d** and two **e** squares.

11 Now sew units **b/c** together with unit **d/e/e**. Take this pieced unit and add the two rectangle pieces **a** to the top and bottom, and press. Set aside for the moment.

12 Follow **Fig H** for sewing the lid. Sew pieces **g**, **h** and **g** together in a row and press. Add piece **i** to the bottom of the unit. Now sew piece **f** to the left-hand side of the unit and piece **j** to the right-hand side, and press. Set the unit aside for the moment.

Fig G Sewing the Block 1 spout

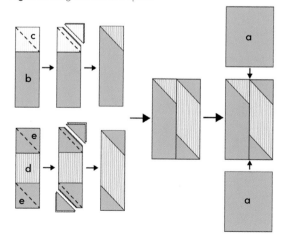

Fig H Sewing the Block 1 lid

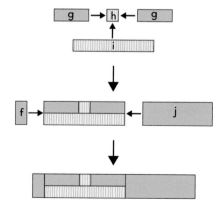

Fig I Sewing the Block 1 body and handle

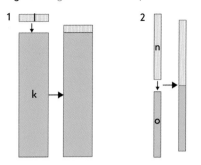

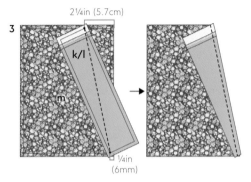

2¼in (5.7cm)

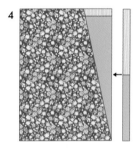

¼in
(6mm)

Fig J Assembling Block 1

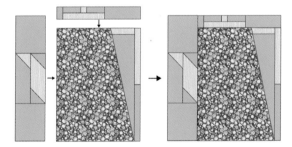

Fig K Sewing a Block 2 body

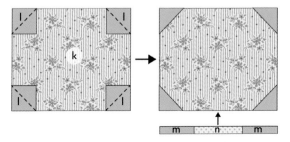

13 Follow **Fig I** for sewing the teapot body and handle. Sew pieces **k** and **l** together and press (**Fig I 1**). Sew pieces **n** and **o** together and press (**Fig I 2**). Take unit **k/l** and on the *wrong* side use an erasable marker to mark the ¼in (6mm) seam allowance all round. On this unit, also mark a diagonal line from corner to corner of the seam allowance (*not* the outer corners of the shape). On the *right* side of piece **m** mark the ¼in (6mm) seam allowance. On piece **m**, mark a dot 2¼in (5.7cm) away from the top right-hand edge of the fabric, as shown on **Fig I 3**. Mark another dot at the bottom right-hand side, on the ¼in (6mm) seam allowance corner.

14 Place unit **k/l** right sides together with piece **m**, angling the narrow unit as shown in the diagram, so the dots match up at the top and bottom. Pin in place and then sew along the marked diagonal line (you can sew to the edges of the fabric). Trim excess fabric ¼in (6mm) away from the sewn line and press the triangle outwards. To complete the body and handle, sew unit **n/o** to the right-hand side.

15 To assemble the block follow **Fig J**. Sew the lid section to the body section and press. Now add the spout section and press. The block should be 10in x 10½in (25.4cm x 26.7cm) at this stage.

16 Make three of Block 1A like this in total. Repeat the process and change fabrics to sew three of Block 1B – see **Fig C** for fabrics used.

MAKING A BLOCK 2 TEAPOT

17 Each Block 2 is made the same way, but in four different colourways (see **Fig C**). Block 2A is described in detail here. **Fig E** shows the layout of the block, with the letters indicating the cut sizes of the fabric pieces. When you have cut all the pieces for one block, lay them out in the different sections of the block as best you can.

18 For the spout, use pieces **b**, **c**, **d**, **e** and **f**, and follow the same basic process as described in the Block 1 teapot (Steps 10–11).

19 For the lid, use pieces **g**, **h**, **i** and **j**, and follow the same basic process as described in the Block 1 teapot (Step 12).

20 For the teapot body following **Fig K**. Take piece **k** and four **l** squares and create triangle corners on the larger piece, using the same technique described for Block 1 (Step 10). For the base of the body, sew two **m** pieces to the sides of an **n** piece. Press and then sew this to the bottom of the body.

21 To make the handle follow the sequence in **Fig L**. Start by sewing the two **q** pieces to the top and bottom of the **p** piece. Press and then add piece **r** to the right-hand side of the unit (**Fig L 1**). The corners **s** and then **t** are created using the same technique described for Block 1 (Step 10) – follow **Fig L 2** and **Fig L 3**. Finally, add piece **o** to the top of the handle and piece **u** to the bottom and press (**Fig L 4**).

22 To assemble the block follow **Fig M**. Sew the spout section and the handle section to the body section and press. Add the long strip of piece **a** to the top of the block. The block should be 14in x 10½in (35.5cm x 26.7cm) at this stage.

23 Make three of Block 2A like this in total. Repeat the process and change fabrics to sew three of Block 2B, 2C and 2D – see **Fig C** for the fabrics used.

MAKING A BLOCK 3 TEAPOT

24 Each Block 3 is made the same way, but in two different colourways (see **Fig C**). Block 3A is described in detail here. **Fig F** shows the layout of the block, with the letters indicating the cut sizes of the fabric pieces. When you have cut all the pieces for one block, lay them out in the different sections of the block as best you can.

25 For the spout, use pieces **a**, **b**, **c**, **d**, **e** and **f**, and follow the same basic process as described in the Block 1 teapot (Steps 10–11).

26 For the lid, use pieces **g**, **h**, **i** and **j**, and follow the same basic process as described in the Block 1 teapot (Step 12).

27 For the teapot body and base use pieces **k**, **l**, **m** and **n**, and follow the same basic process as described in the Block 2 teapot (Step 20).

28 For the handle, use pieces **o**, **p**, **q**, **r**, **s**, **t** and **u**, and follow the same basic process as described in the Block 2 teapot (Step 21).

29 To assemble the block follow **Fig N**. Sew the lid section to the body section and press. Now add the spout section and the handle section and press. The block should be 12in x 10½in (30.5cm x 26.7cm) at this stage.

30 Make three of Block 3A like this in total. Repeat the process and change fabrics to sew three of Block 3B – see **Fig C** for fabrics used.

Fig L Sewing a Block 2 body

Fig M Assembling Block 2

Fig N Assembling Block 3

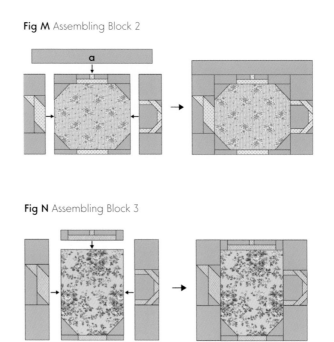

MAKING THE FLYING GEESE ROWS

31 There are seven rows of flying geese units in the quilt – Row 1 is repeated four times and Row 2 repeated three times. Use print fabrics 1, 2, 3, 4, 5, 6, 7 and 8. Each of the flying geese units is made the same way, using the same technique that you used in Block 1 to create the corner triangles. For each unit, use one 4½in x 2½in (11.4cm x 6.4cm) rectangle of print fabric and two 2½in (6.4cm) squares of solid Fabric 15. Follow **Fig O** for the stages of sewing. Each unit needs to be 4½in x 2½in (11.4cm x 6.4cm) unfinished. Make a total of ninety-one units, in the following fabric combinations.

- Fabrics 1 and 15 – make sixteen units.
- Fabrics 2 and 15 – make twelve units.
- Fabrics 3 and 15 – make twelve units.
- Fabrics 4 and 15 – make twelve units.
- Fabrics 5 and 15 – make twelve units.
- Fabrics 6 and 15 – make nine units.
- Fabrics 7 and 15 – make nine units.
- Fabrics 8 and 15 – make nine units.

32 Lay out the flying geese in the order shown in **Fig P**. Note that there are four different units – Unit 1A and 1B, and Unit 2A and 2B. Sew the units together as in the diagram. Repeat the process to make the number of units stated.

33 Now sew the units together into Row 1 and Row 2, as shown in **Fig Q**. Repeat, so you have four of Row 1 and three of Row 2.

ASSEMBLING THE QUILT

34 Lay out the first row of teapot blocks as in **Fig R**. Arrange the 1¼in x 10½in (3.2cm x 26.7cm) vertical sashing pieces in between the blocks and at the ends of the row. Sew the row together. Now follow **Fig B** carefully to sew the rest of the rows, changing the positions of the teapot blocks as shown.

35 When all of the teapot rows are sewn, sew the flying geese rows between each teapot row, and at the top and bottom of the quilt. Ease the rows to fit together neatly, pinning well. Start with flying geese Row 1 at the top, then Row 2 and alternate as in **Fig B**. Press to finish.

QUILTING AND FINISHING

36 Make a quilt sandwich of the backing fabric, wadding (batting) and quilt. Quilt as desired. Square up the quilt, trimming excess wadding and backing.

37 Use the prepared double-fold binding strip to bind your quilt (see Basic Techniques: Binding). Add a label and your quilt is finished.

Fig O Making a flying geese unit

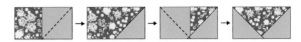

Fig P Sewing the bunting units
Numbers indicate fabrics used

Unit 1A – make 8

Unit 1B – make 4

Unit 2A – make 6

Unit 2B – make 3

Fig Q Sewing the bunting rows together

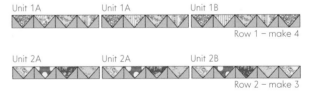

Fig R Sewing a teapot row together

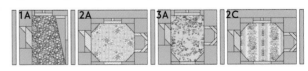

BIRDHOUSE QUILT

This charming quilt uses only two blocks, one a mirror image of the other. It uses mainly teal and yellow fabrics, mostly from the Apple Butter range, and the different fabric combinations give the block a nicely varied look. There is also a version of the quilt using a predominantly blue and red colourway, available at www.tildasworld.com

MATERIALS

- Fabric 1: ¾yd (75cm) – Pen Stripe light blue
- Fabric 2: ½yd (50cm) – Crisscross pink
- Fabric 3: ¾yd (75cm) – Crisscross light blue
- Fabric 4: ½yd (50cm) – Paint Dots light blue
- Fabric 5: ¾yd (75cm) – Tiny Star light blue
- Fabric 6: ¾yd (75cm) – Dottie Dots light blue
- Fabric 7: ½yd (50cm) – Tiny Dots light blue
- Fabric 8: ¼yd (25cm) – Solid cornflower blue
- Fabric 9: ¼yd (25cm) – Shirly teal
- Fabric 10: ¼yd (25cm) – Sue mustard
- Fabric 11: ¼yd (25cm) – Sue dove white
- Fabric 12: ¼yd (25cm) – Billy Jo red
- Fabric 13: ¼yd (25cm) – Nancy yellow
- Fabric 14: ¼yd (25cm) – Bonnie mustard
- Fabric 15: ¼yd (25cm) – Nancy red
- Fabric 16: ¼yd (25cm) – Billy Jo yellow
- Fabric 17: ¼yd (25cm) – Nancy teal
- Fabric 18: ¼yd (25cm) – Medium Dots flaxen yellow
- Backing fabric 3½yd (3.2m)
- Wadding (batting) 60in x 74in (152cm x 188cm)
- Binding fabric ½yd (50cm) – Billy Jo red
- Erasable marker
- Thick card for appliqué templates

Finished Size 52in x 66in (132cm x 168cm)

Fabric Note Where a long quarter of a yard is given in the Materials list you could use a fat quarter instead, assumed to be 21in x 18in (53.3cm x 45.7cm).

Fig A Fabric swatches – if you can't source a fabric, replace with one in a similar colour

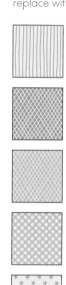

Fabric 1 Pen Stripe light blue

Fabric 2 Crisscross pink

Fabric 3 Crisscross light blue

Fabric 4 Paint Dots light blue

Fabric 5 Tiny Star light blue

Fabric 6 Dottie Dots light blue

Fabric 7 Tiny Dots light blue

Fabric 8 Solid cornflower blue

Fabric 9 Shirly teal

Fabric 10 Sue mustard

Fabric 11 Sue dove white

Fabric 12 Billy Jo red

Fabric 13 Nancy yellow

Fabric 14 Bonnie mustard

Fabric 15 Nancy red

Fabric 16 Billy Jo yellow

Fabric 17 Nancy teal

Fabric 18 Medium Dots flaxen yellow

PREPARATION AND CUTTING OUT

1 Before you start, refer to Basic Techniques: Making Quilts and Pillows. This quilt is made up of two blocks (Block 1 and Block 2), one a mirror image of the other. Block 1 is sewn in two different fabric combinations – 1A and 1B. Block 2 is also sewn in two different fabric combinations – 2A and 2B. The ten prints used for the birdhouse wall varies (piece **i**). There are thirty blocks in total in the quilt, in a 5 x 6 layout. The fabrics used are shown in **Fig A** and the quilt layout in **Fig B**.

2 The exact measurements for cutting out the pieces for Block 1 are given with **Fig C** (they include seam allowances). The Block 2 pieces are exactly the same but the layout of the block is reversed – see **Fig D**. You could cut out all of the pieces at the start, or do it as you make each block. (Be aware that two different **d** squares make two half-square triangle units.) There are nine each of Block 1A and Block 2A in the quilt and six each of Block 1B and Block 2B.

Fig B Quilt layout

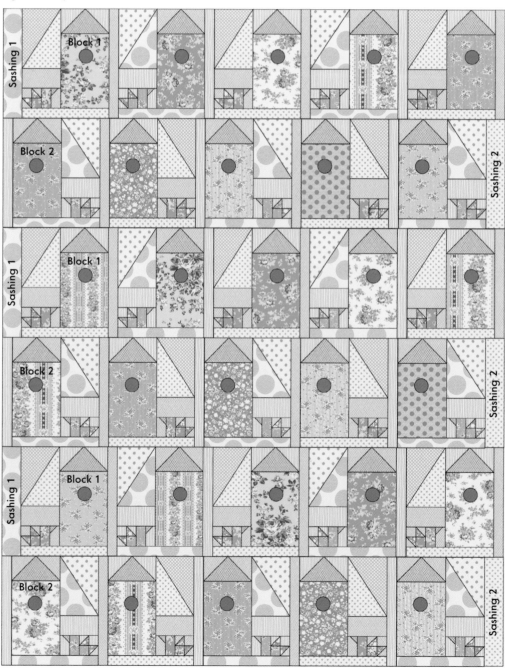

Fig C Block 1 layout and cutting

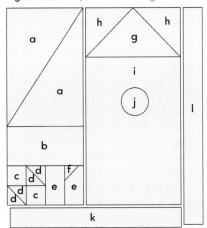

Block 1 (A and B)

a 4½in x 6½in (11.4cm x 16.5cm).
b 4½in x 2½in (11.4cm x 6.4cm).
c 1½in (3.8cm) square.
d 1⅞in (4.8cm) square (one square makes two half-square triangles).
e 1½in x 2½in (3.8cm x 6.4cm).
f 1¼in (3.2cm) square.
g 5½in x 3in (14cm x 7.6cm).
h 3in (7.6cm) square.
i 5½in x 8in (14cm x 20.3cm).
j 2½in (6.4cm) diameter circle for appliqué (see instructions).
k 9½in x 1½in (24.1cm x 3.8cm).
l 1½in x 11½in (3.8cm x 29.2cm).

Fig D Block 2 layout and cutting

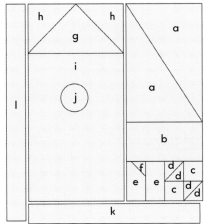

Block 2 (A and B)

Use the same measurements as Block 1: note the layout is reversed

3 The birdhouse wall pieces (piece **i**) are cut 5½in x 8in (14cm x 20.3cm). To make the quilt as shown cut the following rectangles (see **Fig E**). **Fig F** and **Fig G** show the colourways for the blocks.

• Fabric 9 – cut three.
• Fabric 10 – cut three.
• Fabric 11 – cut four.
• Fabric 12 – cut four.
• Fabric 13 – cut four.
• Fabric 14 – cut three.
• Fabric 15 – cut three.
• Fabric 16 – cut two.
• Fabric 17 – cut two.
• Fabric 18 – cut two.

Fig E Fabrics for birdhouse (piece **i**)
Follow **Fig B** for positions of these pieces

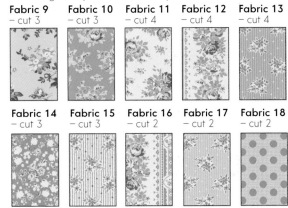

Fabric 9 – cut 3
Fabric 10 – cut 3
Fabric 11 – cut 4
Fabric 12 – cut 4
Fabric 13 – cut 4
Fabric 14 – cut 3
Fabric 15 – cut 3
Fabric 16 – cut 2
Fabric 17 – cut 2
Fabric 18 – cut 2

Fig F Block 1 colourways
Numbers indicate fabrics used

Block 1A – make 9

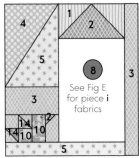

Block 1B – make 6

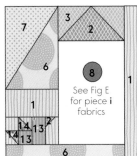

Fig G Block 2 colourways
Numbers indicate fabrics used

Block 2A – make 9 **Block 2B** – make 6

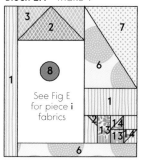
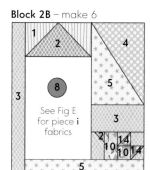

4 For the 'hole' in the birdhouse use solid Fabric 8. Turned-edge appliqué is used for these circles. Cut two strips of fabric about 2¾in (4.4cm) high x width of fabric. From thick card cut a 2½in (6.4cm) diameter circle and a smaller 1½in (3.8cm) diameter circle – you can cut several and re-use them. The appliqué process is described later.

5 Each row of the quilt has one vertical sashing piece at one end of the row, cut 2½in x 11½in (6.4cm x 29.2cm). Cut three pieces from Fabric 5 (Sashing 1) and three from Fabric 6 (Sashing 2).

6 Cut the backing fabric in half across the width. Sew the pieces together along the long side. Press the seam open and trim to a piece about 60in x 74in (152cm x 188cm).

7 From the binding fabric cut seven strips 2½in (6.4cm) x width of fabric. Sew together end to end and press the seams open. Press in half along the length, wrong sides together.

MAKING BLOCK 1

8 A block is made up of different sections, some pieced and some unpieced. We describe making the pieced sections first, describing Block 1A in detail. **Fig H** shows the pieced units. The bird unit contains two half-square triangle units and one corner triangle unit.

Fig H Block 1 pieced sections

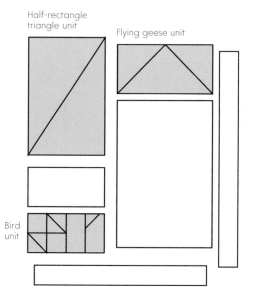

Half-rectangle triangle unit

Flying geese unit

Bird unit

If you want to make them, these delightful Easter hares are available as a free pattern on www.tildasworld.com

9 Making a half-rectangle triangle unit: Take two piece **a** rectangles (for Block 1A this is Fabric 4 and Fabric 5). Use an erasable marker to mark the ¼in (6mm) seam allowance all round on the right side of Fabric 4 and the wrong side of Fabric 5 (**Fig I 1**). (Or just mark a dot at each corner.) On Fabric 5, mark a diagonal line that bisects the seam allowance (*not* the outer corners of the shape). Place the diagonally marked rectangle right sides together with the other rectangle, angling the top piece so the seam allowance dots are aligned as shown in **Fig I 2**. Pin in place and then sew along the marked line (**Fig I 3**) (you can sew to the edges of the fabric). Trim off excess fabric ¼in (6mm) away from the sewn line (**Fig I 4**). Flip the triangle over and press it into place. Check the unit is 5½in x 8in (14cm x 20.3cm).

10 Making half-square triangle units: Two of these half-square triangle (HST) units are needed for each bird. For Block 1A, take a 1⅞in (4.8cm) square (piece **d**) of Fabric 3 and one of Fabric 14. These two squares will make two half-square triangles using the method in Basic Techniques: Half-Square Triangle Units. Once sewn, check each HST unit is 1½in (3.8cm) square.

11 Making a flying geese unit: For each birdhouse roof you will need to make one flying geese unit. Take two **h** squares and one **g**

rectangle – for Block 1A this is Fabric 1 and Fabric 2. Follow the method in Basic Techniques: Flying Geese Unit. Once sewn, check the unit is 5½in x 3in (14cm x 7.6cm).

12 Making a corner triangle unit: This unit creates the beak on the bird. Take one **e** piece and one **f** – for Block 1A this is Fabric 3 and Fabric 2. On the wrong side of piece **f** mark the diagonal line. Place the square right sides together with the rectangle, aligning the top left corners, as shown in **Fig J**. Pin if needed and then sew along the marked line. Trim excess fabric ¼in (6mm) away from the stitching line and press the triangle into place. Check the unit is 1½in x 2½in (3.8cm x 6.4cm).

13 To assemble a bird unit follow **Fig K** to lay out the parts. Sew the **c** squares to the **d** HSTs, as shown. Now sew the units together into a row. Check the unit is 4½in x 2½in (11.4cm x 6.4cm).

14 To make the 'hole' in the birdhouse, make an appliqué circle. Use the large circle card template to cut thirty 2½in (6.4cm) diameter circles from the strips of Fabric 8 cut earlier. This size allows for a generous seam. Now follow the instructions in Basic Techniques: Appliqué: Gathering Over Card Method.

Fig I Making a half-rectangle triangle unit

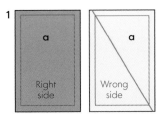

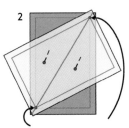

Mark ¼in (6mm) seam allowances and a diagonal line through the seam allowance points of the lighter rectangle

Angle rectangle so seam allowance points meet marked lines beneath

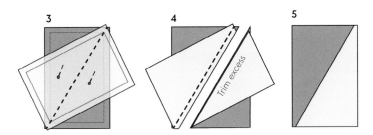

Fig J Making a corner triangle unit

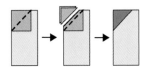

Fig K Assembling a bird unit

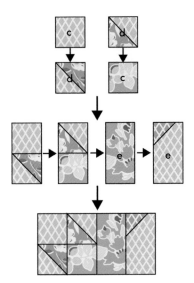

15 Place the appliqué circle on to piece **i** of the birdhouse, positioning it in the centre and about 1¾in (4.4cm) down from the raw top edge. Sew into place with matching thread and tiny stitches. Use this process to make and sew circles for all the blocks.

16 To assemble Block 1A, take the pieced units for the block and with the unpieced units, lay out the parts as in **Fig L**. Start by sewing the units into columns. Sew the two columns together and press. Add piece **k** to the bottom of the block and press. Add piece **l** to the right-hand side and press. Check the block is 10½in x 11½in (26.7cm x 29.2cm).

17 Repeat this process to make a total of nine of Block 1A and six of Block 1B, changing the birdhouse wall fabric as shown in **Fig B**.

18 Repeat this process to make nine of Block 2A and six of Block 2B, changing the birdhouse wall fabric as needed. Remember that the layout for Block 2 is a mirror image of Block 1 (see **Fig D**).

ASSEMBLING THE QUILT

19 Follow **Fig B** carefully, laying out the blocks as shown. **Fig M** shows the first two rows of the quilt in more detail. For Row 1, sew five of Block 1 together in a row, alternating A and B blocks, pressing the seams in one direction. Add a Sashing 1 piece of Fabric 6 to the left-hand side of the row. For Row 2, sew five of Block 2 together in a row, alternating A and B blocks, pressing the seams in the opposite direction to Row 1. Add a Sashing 2 piece of Fabric 5 to the right-hand side of the row. Continue in this way to sew all the rows of the quilt. Now sew the rows together, matching seams neatly where needed, and press.

QUILTING AND FINISHING

20 Make a quilt sandwich of the backing fabric, wadding (batting) and quilt. Quilt as desired. Square up the quilt, trimming excess wadding and backing.

21 Use the prepared double-fold binding strip to bind your quilt (see Basic Techniques: Binding). Add a label and your quilt is finished.

Fig L Assembling Block 1A

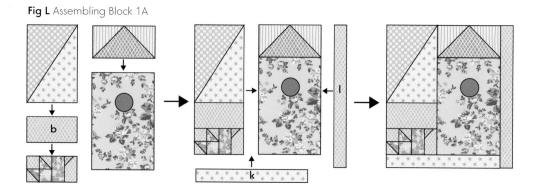

Fig M Assembling quilt rows 1 and 2

Row 1

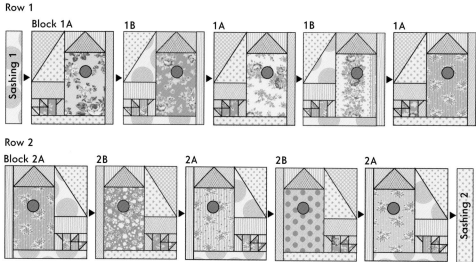

Row 2

FAN FLOWER QUILT

This fun quilt features bold flowers created using an easy Dresden wedge technique for the petals, plus a simple leaf block made from half-rectangle triangle units. Some turned-edge appliqué adds to the charming look. The quilt uses mainly blue and coral fabrics, mostly from the Lazy Days range. There is also a version that uses predominantly pink and green colours (see www.tildasworld.com).

MATERIALS

- Fabric 1: 1yd (1m) – Solid lilac
- Fabric 2: 1yd (1m) – Solid night blue
- Fabric 3: 1yd (1m) – Solid salmon
- Fabric 4: 1⅛yd (1.2m) – Pen Stripe grey
- Fabric 5: ¼yd (25cm) – Josephine sand
- Fabric 6: ¼yd (25cm) – Phoebe ginger
- Fabric 7: ¼yd (25cm) – Mildred ginger
- Fabric 8: ¼yd (25cm) – Eleanore coral
- Fabric 9: ¼yd (25cm) – Frances pink
- Fabric 10: ⅜yd (40cm) – Trickles teal
- Fabric 11: ¼yd (25cm) – Eleanore teal
- Fabric 12: ¼yd (25cm) – Josephine teal
- Fabric 13: ¼yd (25cm) – Phoebe emerald
- Fabric 14: ¼yd (25cm) – Mildred green
- Fabric 15: ¼yd (25cm) – Frances teal
- Fabric 16: ⅜yd (40cm) – Trickles coral
- Fabric 17: ¼yd (25cm) – Eleanore lilac
- Fabric 18: ⅜yd (40cm) – Josephine emerald
- Fabric 19: ¼yd (25cm) – Frances lilac
- Fabric 20: ¼yd (25cm) – Phoebe thistle
- Fabric 21: 8in (20.3cm) square – Mildred lilac
- Fabric 22: ⅜yd (40cm) – Trickles blue
- Fabric 23: ¼yd (25cm) – Frances blue
- Fabric 24: ¼yd (25cm) – Eleanore blue
- Fabric 25: ¼yd (25cm) – Mildred blue
- Fabric 26: ⅜yd (40cm) – Josephine blue
- Fabric 27: 8in (20.3cm) square – Phoebe blue
- Fabric 28: ⅜yd (40cm) – Trickles lilac
- Backing fabric 3⅝yd (3.3m)
- Wadding (batting) 64in x 79in (163cm x 200cm)
- Binding fabric ½yd (50cm) – Solid lime green
- Erasable marker
- Thick card for templates

Finished Size 55in x 70in (140cm x 178cm)

Fig A Fabric swatches – if you can't source a fabric, replace with one in a similar colour

Fabric 1 Solid lilac

Fabric 11 Eleanore teal

Fabric 21 Mildred lilac

Fabric 2 Solid night blue

Fabric 12 Josephine teal

Fabric 22 Trickles blue

Fabric 3 Solid salmon

Fabric 13 Phoebe emerald

Fabric 23 Frances blue

Fabric 4 Pen Stripe grey

Fabric 14 Mildred green

Fabric 24 Eleanore blue

Fabric 5 Josephine sand

Fabric 15 Frances teal

Fabric 25 Mildred blue

Fabric 6 Phoebe ginger

Fabric 16 Trickles coral

Fabric 26 Josephine blue

Fabric 7 Mildred ginger

Fabric 17 Eleanore lilac

Fabric 27 Phoebe blue

Fabric 8 Eleanore coral

Fabric 18 Josephine emerald

Fabric 28 Trickles lilac

Fabric 9 Frances pink

Fabric 19 Frances lilac

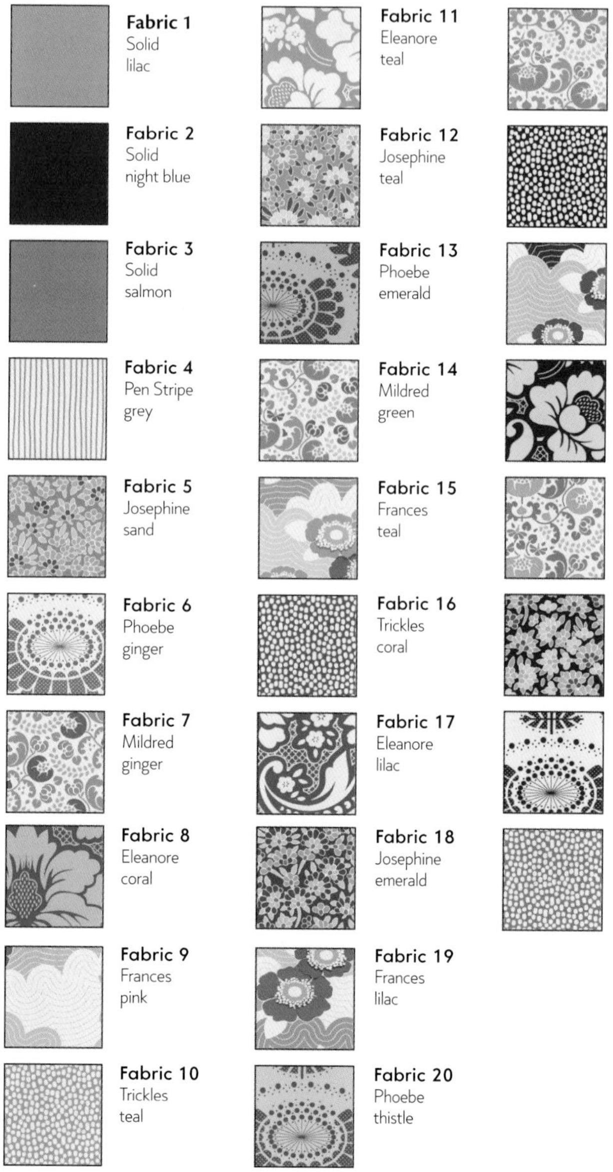

Fabric 10 Trickles teal

Fabric 20 Phoebe thistle

Fabric Note Where a long quarter of a yard is given in the Materials list you could use a fat quarter instead, approximately 21in x 18in (53.3cm x 45.7cm).

PREPARATION AND CUTTING OUT

1 Before you start, refer to Basic Techniques: Making Quilts and Pillows. This quilt is made up of two blocks, a Flower block and a Leaf block, each sewn in four different fabric combinations. Vertical sashing strips bring each row of the quilt up to the same size. The fabrics used are shown in **Fig A** and the quilt layout in **Fig B**.

2 Each Flower block has two pieces of background fabric, **a** and **b** – see **Fig C** for the layout and sizes. The flower petals are cut using a petal template (pattern) from a fabric strip 7¼in (18.4cm) high. The circle is made using turned-edge appliqué. The fabrics used for the four colourways of the Flower block are shown in **Fig D**. A list of the cut pieces needed for one block is given in Making a Flower Block (Step 8).

3 Each Leaf block is made up of rectangles (**c**) cut 5½in x 2½in (14cm x 6.4cm) – see **Fig E** for layout and sizes. Each block needs ten rectangles of background fabric, three rectangles from one print fabric and three rectangles from another print. Some of the

rectangles are used to make half-rectangle triangle (HRT) units. The centre stem (**d**) is made from an appliqué strip. The fabrics used for the four block colourways are shown in **Fig F**. A list of the cut pieces needed for one block is given in Making a Leaf Block (Step 16).

4 For the sashing, cut strips 3½in x 10½in (9cm x 26.7cm), cutting two each from Fabric 1, Fabric 2 and Fabric 4, and one from Fabric 3.

5 Cut the backing fabric in half across the width. Sew the pieces together along the long side. Press the seam open and trim to a piece about 64in x 79in (163cm x 200cm).

6 From the binding fabric cut seven strips 2½in (6.4cm) x width of fabric. Sew together end to end and press the seams open. Press in half along the length, wrong sides together.

7 Copy the petal template and the small and large circle templates onto thick card and cut out the shapes.

Fig B Quilt layout

MAKING A FLOWER BLOCK

8 All of the Flower blocks are made the same way. Instructions and diagrams are given for making a Flower block 1. For one Flower block 1 you will need the following pieces (see also **Fig C** and **Fig D**).

- From Fabric 1, one background piece **a** – 16½in x 8⅝in (42cm x 22.5cm).
- From Fabric 1, one background piece **b** – 16½in x 2⅜in (42cm x 6cm).
- From Fabric 5, two petals, cut using the petal template (see next step).
- From Fabric 6, two petals.
- From Fabric 7, two petals.
- From Fabric 8, two petals.
- From Fabric 9, one petal.
- From Fabric 10, one circle, cut using the large circle template.

Fig C Flower block layout and cutting

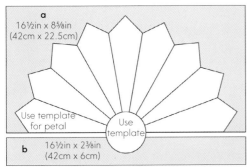

Fig D Flower block colourways
Numbers indicate fabrics

Flower block 1
– make 4

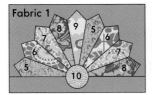

Flower block 2
– make 4

Flower block 3
– make 3

Flower block 4
– make 3

Fig E Leaf block layout and cutting

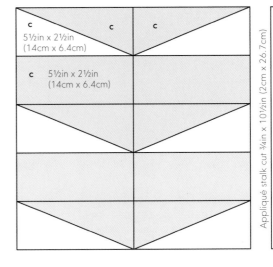

41

9 To cut petals, take a 7¼in (18.4cm) high fabric strip, place the petal template on the fabric and mark the shape (**Fig G**). Rotate the template 180 degrees and mark another shape. Use a normal quilting ruler to cut out the shapes accurately. Repeat this process with the other fabrics to cut the petals needed.

10 To create a petal follow the sequence in **Fig H**. Take a petal, fold the shape in half vertically, right sides together and align the top edges. Sew a ¼in (6mm) seam along the top. Trim a small triangle from the seam allowance. Open up the top of the petal and press the seam open. Turn the petal right side out, poke out the top point with a pointed stick or similar tool and then press again. Repeat this to make all nine petals for one Flower block 1.

11 Lay out the nine petals in the order shown in **Fig D**. Take the first two petals, place them right sides together and sew the side seam. Press the seam open or to one side. Continue like this, sewing all of the petals together and then press (**Fig I**).

12 To assemble the block, take a 16½in x 8⅝in (42cm x 22.5cm) piece of Fabric 1, fold it in half vertically and press a light crease. Position the petal unit on the fabric, lining up the centre of the petal unit with the creased line and with the bottom edges aligned, as in **Fig J**. Pin the petal unit in position. Take a 16½in x 2⅜in (42cm x 6cm) piece of Fabric 1, place it right sides together with the bottom of the block, as shown. Sew together using a ¼in (6mm) seam and press.

Fig G Marking petals using the template

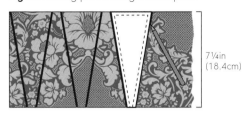

7¼in (18.4cm)

Fig H Making a petal

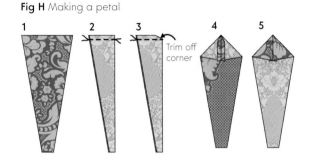

Trim off corner

1 2 3 4 5

Fig I Sewing the petals together

Fig F Leaf block colourways
Numbers indicate fabrics

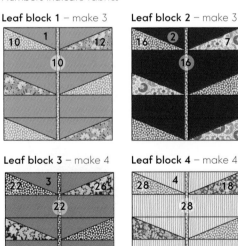

Leaf block 1 – make 3

10 1 12
10

Leaf block 2 – make 3

16 2 7
16

Leaf block 3 – make 4

22 3 26
22

Leaf block 4 – make 4

28 4 18
28

Fig J Assembling a Flower block

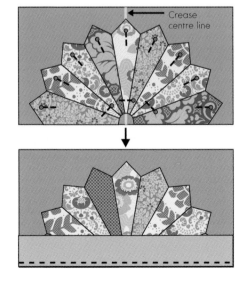

Crease centre line

13 Make an appliqué circle following the stages in **Fig K**. Use the large circle template to cut a 4in (10.2cm) diameter circle from Fabric 10 (for Flower block 1). This allows for a seam of about ¾in (2cm) all round. Place the smaller circle template in the centre of a fabric circle and use a pencil to mark the circle. Use a doubled thread to sew a circle of gathering stitches about ⅛in (3mm) *outside* of the marked line. Place the small card circle back onto the fabric and pin in place. Pull up the gathering threads, to gather the fabric around the card. Tie off the threads and press. Remove the card and press again. You can leave the gathering in place if it doesn't show.

14 Place the appliqué circle onto the block, in the position shown in **Fig L**. Sew the petal unit and the circle into place using matching thread and tiny stitches around the edges of the shapes. Press the block and check it is 16½in x 10½in (42cm x 26.7cm). Repeat this process to make a total of four Flower block 1.

15 Repeat this whole process to make the rest of the Flower blocks, following the fabrics and numbers of blocks in **Fig D**.

MAKING A LEAF BLOCK
16 All of the Leaf blocks are made the same way. Instructions and diagrams are given for making a Leaf block 1. For one Leaf block 1 you will need the following pieces (see also **Fig E** and **Fig F**).

- From Fabric 1, four of piece **c** – 5½in x 2½in (14cm x 6.4cm).
- From Fabric 1, six of piece **c** for HRT units.
- From Fabric 10, three of piece **c** for HRT units.
- From Fabric 12, three of piece **c** for HRT units.
- From Fabric 10, one strip **d** for a stem – ¾in x 10½in (2cm x 26.7cm).

17 To make a half-rectangle triangle unit, take a 5½in x 2½in (14cm x 6.4cm) rectangle of Fabric 1 and of Fabric 10. Use an erasable marker to mark the ¼in (6mm) seam allowance all round on the right side (RS) of Fabric 1 and the wrong side (WS) of Fabric 10 (see **Fig M 1**). On Fabric 10, mark a diagonal line that bisects the seam allowance (*not* the outer corners of the shape). Place the diagonally marked rectangle right sides together with the other rectangle, angling the top piece so the seam allowance corners are aligned as in **Fig M 2**. Pin in place and then sew along the marked line (you can sew to the edges of the fabric if you like). Trim off excess fabric ¼in (6mm) away from the sewn line (**Fig M 3**). Flip the triangle over and press it into place. Check the unit is 5½in x 2½in (14cm x 6.4cm).

18 Make another HRT like this using Fabrics 1 and 10 and then make one unit using Fabrics 1 and 12.

Fig K Making an appliqué circle

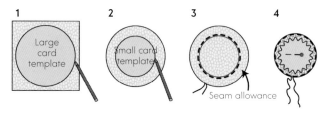

Fig L Sewing the appliqués in place

Fig M Making a half-rectangle triangle unit

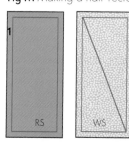

Mark ¼in (6mm) seam allowances and a diagonal line through the seam allowance points of the print rectangle

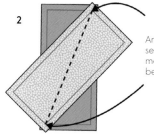

Angle the rectangle so seam allowance points meet marked corners beneath and then sew

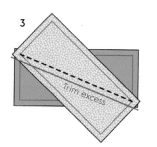
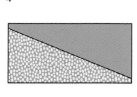

19 Make three more HRT units for the other half of the block (one with Fabrics 1 and 10 and two with Fabrics 1 and 12). These units have to face the *opposite* way, so draw the diagonal line facing the opposite way, and angle the top piece the opposite way, so the final unit will have its diagonal line slanting in the opposite direction.

20 Lay out the ten units for the block as in **Fig N**. Sew them together in columns and then sew the columns together and press. Check the block is 10½in (26.7cm) square.

21 For the stem, take a ¾in x 10½in (2cm x 26.7cm) strip of Fabric 10. Fold each long edge over to the wrong side by ¼in (6mm) and press. Now fold the strip in half along the length, so it is about ¼in (6mm) wide and press. Sew the stem into place down the centre of the block using matching thread and tiny stitches along the long edges and press.

22 Repeat this process to make the rest of the Leaf blocks, following the fabrics and numbers of blocks given in **Fig F**.

ASSEMBLING THE QUILT

23 Take the Flower blocks, the Leaf blocks and the seven 3½in x 10½in (9cm x 26.7cm) sashing pieces. Lay out the first four rows of the quilt as shown in **Fig O**. Sew each row together, pressing the seams of Rows 1 and 3 in the opposite direction to Rows 2 and 4. Now sew the four rows together and press. Add the remaining three rows in the same way, following the layout in **Fig B** (the first three rows, repeated).

QUILTING AND FINISHING

24 Make a quilt sandwich of the backing fabric, wadding (batting) and quilt. Quilt as desired. Square up the quilt, trimming excess wadding and backing.

25 Use the prepared double-fold binding strip to bind your quilt (see Basic Techniques: Binding). Add a label and your quilt is finished.

Fig N Assembling a Leaf block

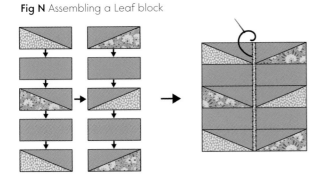

Fig O Assembling the quilt rows

Row 1

Row 2

Row 3

Row 4

FOUR BLOCK QUILT

This pretty quilt uses four blocks, but in different colourways to take advantage of many of the lovely fabrics in the Lazy Days fabric collection. The block is an easy one and creates an eight-point star pattern. The quilt described here uses mainly lilac and teal fabrics. There is another version of the quilt that uses predominantly red and blue fabrics (see www.tildasworld.com). There is also a matching pillow design (described in the next chapter).

MATERIALS

- Fabric 1: ½yd (50cm) – Frances lilac
- Fabric 2: ½yd (50cm) – Medium Dots lilac
- Fabric 3: ½yd (50cm) – Eleanore teal
- Fabric 4: ¼yd (25cm) – Mildred green
- Fabric 5: ⅝yd (60cm) – Tiny Dots light blue
- Fabric 6: ¼yd (25cm) – Josephine emerald
- Fabric 7: ¼yd (25cm) – Eleanore lilac
- Fabric 8: ⅛yd (15cm) – Luna teal sage
  (see Fabric Note, below)
- Fabric 9: ⅝yd (60cm) – Tiny Star light blue
- Fabric 10: ¼yd (25cm) – Trickles lilac
- Fabric 11: ¼yd (25cm) – Phoebe emerald
- Fabric 12: ¼yd (25cm) – Josephine teal
- Fabric 13: ⅝yd (60cm) – Pen Stripe light blue
- Fabric 14: ¼yd (25cm) – Frances teal
- Fabric 15: ¼yd (25cm) – Phoebe thistle
- Fabric 16: ⅝yd (60cm) – Crisscross light blue
- Fabric 17: ⅛yd (15cm) or 10in (25.4cm) square – Trickles green
- Fabric 18: ⅛yd (15cm) or 10in (25.4cm) square – Mildred lilac
- Backing fabric 3½yd (3.2m)
- Wadding (batting) 63in x 77in (160cm x 195.5cm)
- Binding fabric ½yd (50cm) – Dottie Dots light blue

Finished Size 54in x 68in (137cm x 173cm)

Fig A Fabric swatches – if you can't source a fabric, replace with one in a similar colour

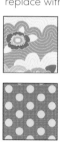
Fabric 1
Frances
lilac

Fabric 8
Luna
teal sage

Fabric 15
Phoebe
thistle

Fabric 2
Medium Dots
lilac

Fabric 9
Tiny Star
light blue

Fabric 16
Crisscross
light blue

Fabric 3
Eleanore
teal

Fabric 10
Trickles
lilac

Fabric 17
Trickles
green

Fabric 4
Mildred
green

Fabric 11
Phoebe
emerald

Fabric 18
Mildred
lilac

Fabric 5
Tiny Dots
light blue

Fabric 12
Josephine
teal

Fabric 6
Josephine
emerald

Fabric 13
Pen Stripe
light blue

Fabric 7
Eleanore
lilac

Fabric 14
Frances
teal

Fabric Note Where a long eighth or long quarter of a yard is given in the Materials list you could use fat eighths and fat quarters instead. A fat eighth is 10½in x 18in (26.7cm x 45.7cm) and a fat quarter 21in x 18in (53.3cm x 45.7cm). However, Fabric 8, Luna teal sage is 108in (274cm) wide, so use only a long eighth, to avoid wastage.

PREPARATION AND CUTTING OUT

1 Before you start, refer to Basic Techniques: Making Quilts and Pillows. This quilt is made up of a single block layout in four different colour combinations, called Block 1, Block 2, Block 3 and Block 4. There are twenty blocks in total, in a 4 x 5 arrangement, separated by sashing strips and corner posts (corner squares). The fabrics used are shown in **Fig A** and the quilt layout in **Fig B**.

2 The block layout and the exact measurements for cutting out the pieces are given with **Fig C** (seam allowances are included). The four different colourways are shown in **Fig D**.

3 Cutting for Block 1: For *each* Block 1 cut the following pieces.
• From Fabric 1 cut four 3½in (9cm) squares (**a**).
• From Fabric 2 cut four 3½in (9cm) squares (**a**).
• From Fabric 3 cut four 3½in (9cm) squares (**b**), for flying geese units.
• From Fabric 4 cut four 3½in (9cm) squares (**b**), for flying geese units.
• From Fabric 5 cut four 6½in x 3½in (16.5cm x 9cm) rectangles (**c**), for flying geese units.

Fig B Quilt layout

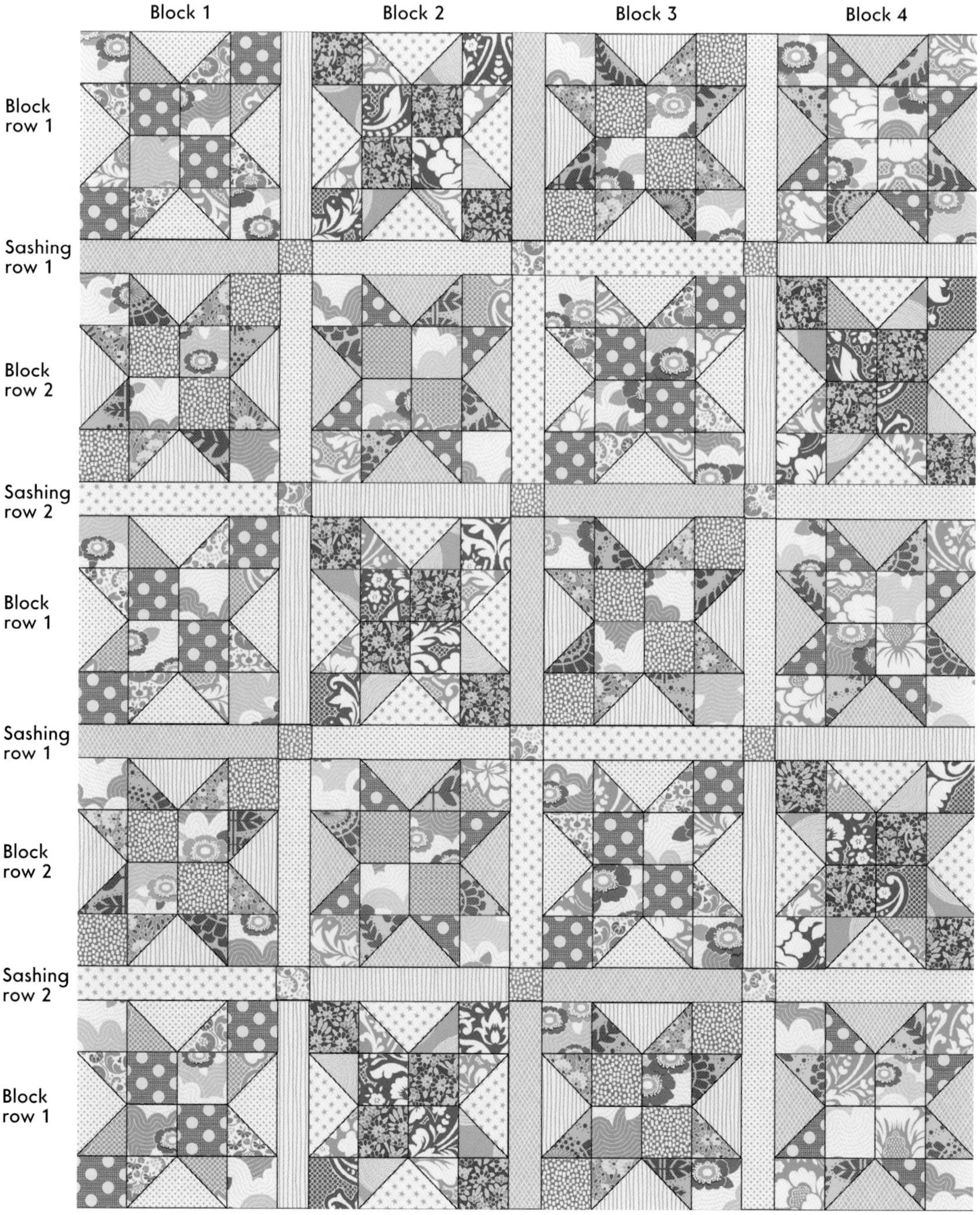

Block 1   Block 2   Block 3   Block 4

Block row 1
Sashing row 1
Block row 2
Sashing row 2
Block row 1
Sashing row 1
Block row 2
Sashing row 2
Block row 1

4 Cutting for Block 2: Cut as Block 1 but use Fabrics 6, 7, 3, 8 and 9 (see **Fig D**).

5 Cutting for Block 3: Cut as Block 1 but use Fabrics 1, 10, 11, 12 and 13 (see **Fig D**).

6 Cutting for Block 4: Cut as Block 1 but use Fabrics 14, 3, 2, 15 and 16 (see **Fig D**).

7 Cutting the sashing: Cut the following pieces (see **Fig E**).
• For Sashing 1, from Fabric 13 cut nine 12½in x 2½in (31.8cm x 6.4cm) strips.
• For Sashing 2, from Fabric 16 cut seven 12½in x 2½in (31.8cm x 6.4cm) strips.
• For Sashing 3, from Fabric 5 cut nine 12½in x 2½in (31.8cm x 6.4cm) strips.
• For Sashing 4, from Fabric 9 cut six 12½in x 2½in (31.8cm x 6.4cm) strips.
• For Corner Post 1, from Fabric 17 cut six 2½in (6.4cm) squares.
• For Corner Post 2, from Fabric 18 cut six 2½in (6.4cm) squares.

8 Cut the backing fabric in half across the width. Sew the pieces together along the long side. Press the seam open and trim to a piece about 63in x 77in (160cm x 195.5cm).

9 From the binding fabric cut seven strips 2½in (6.4cm) x width of fabric. Sew together end to end and press the seams open. Press in half along the length, wrong sides together.

MAKING BLOCK 1

10 All of the blocks are made in the same way. Detailed instructions are given for Block 1. Start by making a flying geese unit, as follows. Take one square of Fabric 3, one square of Fabric 4 and one rectangle of Fabric 5. On the wrong side of the two squares, draw a diagonal line with a pencil. Place a small square right sides together with the rectangle, aligning the corners as shown in **Fig F**, and with the marked line as shown. Pin together if needed. Sew along the line. Trim excess fabric ¼in (6mm) away from the stitching line and press the triangle into place. Sew the second square to the rectangle in the same way on the opposite side and press. Repeat this process to make four flying geese units in total for one Block 1.

Fig C Block layout and cutting

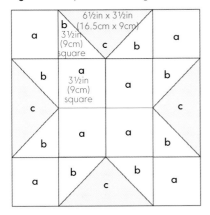

Fig D Block colourways
Numbers indicate fabrics – make 5 of each block

Block 1

Block 2

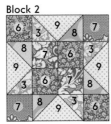

Block 3

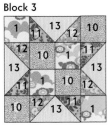

Block 4

Fig E Sashing cutting and fabrics used

Sashing 1 – From Fabric 13 cut nine

12½in x 2½in (31.8cm x 6.4cm)

Sashing 2 – From Fabric 16 cut seven

Sashing 3 – From Fabric 5 cut nine

Sashing 4 – From Fabric 9 cut six

Corner Post 1
From Fabric 17
cut six

2½in (6.4cm)

Corner Post 2
From Fabric 18
cut six

2½in (6.4cm)

Fig F Making a flying geese unit

11 Now make the four-patch unit for the centre of the block. Take two squares of Fabric 1 and two squares of Fabric 2 and arrange them as shown in **Fig G**. Sew them together in pairs and press. Sew the two pairs together and press.

12 Take the nine units for Block 1 and lay them out as **Fig H**, making sure you place the corner squares in the correct positions and have the flying geese units with the points facing inwards. Sew the units together in three rows, pressing the seams of the top and bottom rows in the opposite direction to the middle row. Now sew the rows together, aligning seams neatly, and press. Check the block is 12½in (31.8cm) square at this stage. Repeat this process to make a total of five of Block 1.

13 Repeat the block-making process but changing fabrics as shown in **Fig D**, to make five each of Block 2, Block 3 and Block 4.

ASSEMBLING THE QUILT
14 The quilt is made up of two block rows and two sashing rows, and these rows are repeated down the length of the quilt, finishing with block row 1. Begin sewing the quilt together by carefully laying out these rows as shown in **Fig I**.

For block row 1, arrange Blocks 1, 2, 3 and 4 with sashing strips 1, 2 and 3 between the blocks. Sew the row together and press.

For sashing row 1, arrange sashing strips 2, 3, 4 and 1, with corner post squares 1, 2 and 1 between the strips, as shown. Sew the row together and press the seams in the opposite direction to block row 1.

15 Repeat this process to sew block row 2 and sashing row 2, following the positions of the units as shown in **Fig I**. Now sew these four rows together as in **Fig J**, taking care to align seams neatly. Continue like this to assemble the rest of the quilt, as in **Fig B**.

QUILTING AND FINISHING
16 Make a quilt sandwich of the backing fabric, wadding (batting) and quilt. Quilt as desired. Square up the quilt, trimming excess wadding and backing.

17 Use the prepared double-fold binding strip to bind your quilt (see Basic Techniques: Binding). Add a label and your quilt is finished.

Fig G Making the block centre

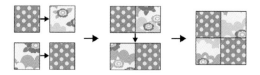

Fig H Assembling a block

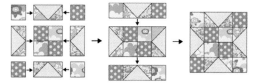

Fig I Assembling the quilt rows

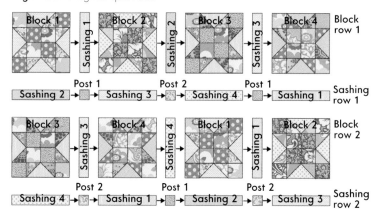

Fig J Joining the rows

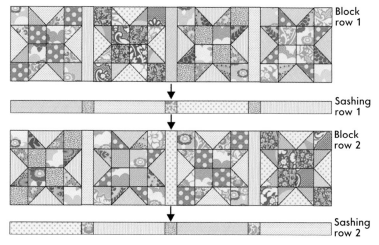

FOUR BLOCK PILLOW

This pillow is the perfect companion to the Four Block Quilt, as it uses the same blocks and the same lilac and teal colours. A red/blue version of the pillow is also available (for details see www.tildasworld.com). Only small amounts of fabric are needed. Refer to the fabric swatches in **Fig A** of the quilt instructions. A fat eighth is approximately 10½in x 18in (26.7cm x 45.7cm).

MATERIALS

- Fabric 1: 12in (30.5cm) square or fat eighth – Frances lilac
- Fabric 2: 12in (30.5cm) square or fat eighth – Medium Dots lilac
- Fabric 3: ⅛yd (15cm) or fat eighth – Eleanore teal
- Fabric 4: 10in (25.4cm) square – Mildred green
- Fabric 5: ⅛yd (15cm) or fat eighth – Tiny Dots light blue
- Fabric 6: 10in (25.4cm) square – Josephine emerald
- Fabric 7: 10in (25.4cm) square – Eleanore lilac
- Fabric 8: 10in (25.4cm) square – Luna teal sage (this fabric is 108in/274cm wide)
- Fabric 9: ⅛yd (15cm) or fat eighth – Tiny Star light blue
- Fabric 10: 10in (25.4cm) square – Trickles lilac
- Fabric 11: 10in (25.4cm) square – Phoebe emerald
- Fabric 12: 10in (25.4cm) square – Josephine teal
- Fabric 13: ⅛yd (15cm) or fat eighth – Pen Stripe light blue
- Fabric 14: 10in (25.4cm) square – Frances teal
- Fabric 15: 10in (25.4cm) square – Phoebe thistle
- Fabric 16: ⅛yd (15cm) or fat eighth – Crisscross light blue
- Fabric 17: 2½in (6.4cm) square – Trickles green
- Lining fabric (optional) 30in (76.2cm) square
- Fabric for pillow back, two pieces 17in x 26½in (43.2cm x 67.3cm)
- Wadding (batting) 30in (76.2cm) square
- Binding fabric ¼yd (25cm) – Dottie Dots light blue
- Pillow pad to fit cover

Finished Size 26in x 26in (66cm x 66cm)

PREPARATION AND CUTTING OUT

1 The cutting for the blocks is the same as the quilt, but only one of each block is needed. Follow the instructions and diagrams for the quilt – you will need the same 3½in (9cm) squares and 6½in x 3½in (16.5cm x 9cm) rectangles.

2 For the sashing, cut one 12½in x 2½in (31.8cm x 6.4cm) strip from Fabric 13, 16, 5 and 9. Cut one 2½in (6.4cm) square from Fabric 17.

3 From binding fabric cut three strips 2½in (6.4cm) x width of fabric. Sew together and press seams open. Press in half along the length, wrong sides together.

MAKING THE BLOCKS AND ASSEMBLING THE PILLOW

4 Make each block following the instructions for the quilt, Steps 10 to 13.

5 Lay out the four blocks, the four sashing strips and the corner post square as in **Fig A** here. Sew the units together in rows and then sew the rows together, matching seams neatly. Press the patchwork, which should be 26½in (67.3cm) square.

QUILTING AND MAKING UP

6 Make a quilt sandwich of the patchwork, wadding (batting) and lining fabric (if using). Quilt as desired. Trim excess wadding and lining to match the patchwork size.

7 To make up the pillow cover, follow the instructions in Basic Techniques: Bound-Edge Pillow Cover. Insert a pillow pad to finish.

Fig A Assembling the pillow

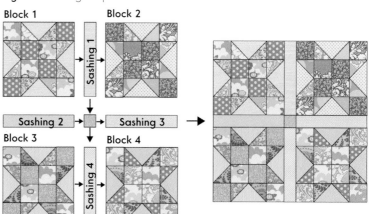

CAT AND BIRD QUILT

This adorable quilt is irresistible, especially if you are a cat-lover. The curved shape for the cat's back is easy to sew using the patterns provided. The cheeks and noses are made using turned-edge appliqué.

MATERIALS

- Fabric 1: ¾yd (75cm) – Pen Stripe light blue
- Fabric 2: ⅜yd (40cm) – Frances pink
- Fabric 3: ⅜yd (40cm) – Phoebe ginger
- Fabric 4: ¼yd (25cm) – Trickles coral
- Fabric 5: ⅛yd (15cm) – Medium Dots salmon
- Fabric 6: ¾yd (75cm) – Paint Dots light blue
- Fabric 7: ⅛yd (15cm) – Medium Dots night blue
- Fabric 8: ½yd (50cm) – Dottie Dots light blue
- Fabric 9: ⅜yd (40cm) – Eleanore lilac
- Fabric 10: ¼yd (25cm) – Mildred lilac
- Fabric 11: ¼yd (25cm) – Trickles lilac
- Fabric 12: ⅛yd (15cm) – Medium Dots dark teal
- Fabric 13: ¼yd (25cm) – Phoebe blue
- Fabric 14: 10in (25.4cm) square – Trickles blue
- Fabric 15: ⅜yd (40cm) – Josephine blue
- Fabric 16: ⅛yd (15cm) – Medium Dots ginger
- Fabric 17: ⅝yd (60cm) – Tiny Star light blue
- Fabric 18: 10in (25.4cm) – Frances lilac
- Fabric 19: ⅝yd (60cm) – Crisscross light blue
- Fabric 20: ⅛yd (15cm) – Phoebe thistle
- Fabric 21: ¼yd (25cm) – Josephine emerald
- Fabric 22: 6in (15.2cm) square – Frances blue
- Fabric 23: 10in (25.4cm) square – Mildred ginger
- Fabric 24: ⅛yd (15cm) – Eleanore coral
- Fabric 25: 10in (25.4cm) square – Phoebe emerald
- Fabric 26: 6in (15.2cm) square – Eleanore teal
- Fabric 27: ¼yd (25cm) – Tiny Dots light blue *
- Fabric 28: ⅜yd (40cm) – Trickles teal
- Fabric 29: ⅝yd (60cm) – Solid warm sand
- Fabric 30: 10in (25.4cm) square – Solid dusty rose
- Fabric 31: 10in (25.4cm) square – Solid salmon
- Fabric 32: 6in (15.2cm) square – Solid pale yellow
- Backing fabric 3½yd (3.2m)
- Wadding (batting) 61in x 82in (155cm x 208cm)
- Binding fabric ½yd (50cm) – Solid lime green
- Black embroidery cotton (floss) for eyes
- Thick card and thick paper for patterns
- Fabric glue for paper piece appliqué

Fig A Fabric swatches – if you can't source a fabric, replace with one in a similar colour

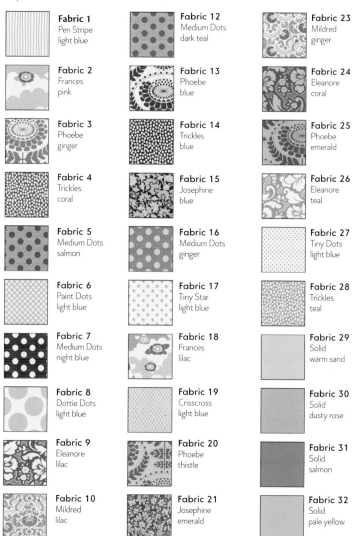

Fabric 1 Pen Stripe light blue
Fabric 2 Frances pink
Fabric 3 Phoebe ginger
Fabric 4 Trickles coral
Fabric 5 Medium Dots salmon
Fabric 6 Paint Dots light blue
Fabric 7 Medium Dots night blue
Fabric 8 Dottie Dots light blue
Fabric 9 Eleanore lilac
Fabric 10 Mildred lilac
Fabric 11 Trickles lilac
Fabric 12 Medium Dots dark teal
Fabric 13 Phoebe blue
Fabric 14 Trickles blue
Fabric 15 Josephine blue
Fabric 16 Medium Dots ginger
Fabric 17 Tiny Star light blue
Fabric 18 Frances lilac
Fabric 19 Crisscross light blue
Fabric 20 Phoebe thistle
Fabric 21 Josephine emerald
Fabric 22 Frances blue
Fabric 23 Mildred ginger
Fabric 24 Eleanore coral
Fabric 25 Phoebe emerald
Fabric 26 Eleanore teal
Fabric 27 Tiny Dots light blue
Fabric 28 Trickles teal
Fabric 29 Solid warm sand
Fabric 30 Solid dusty rose
Fabric 31 Solid salmon
Fabric 32 Solid pale yellow

Finished Size 52½in x 73½in (133.3cm x 186.7cm)

Fabric Note Where a long eighth or long quarter of a yard is given in the Materials list you could use fat eighths and fat quarters instead (* except Fabric 27, which must be a long ¼yd). A fat eighth is approximately 10½in x 18in (26.7cm x 45.7cm) and a fat quarter 21in x 18in (53.3cm x 45.7cm). Take care to cut your fabrics as economically as possible: some of the tall shapes can be cut horizontally on the fabric if desired.

PREPARATION AND CUTTING OUT

1 Before you start, refer to Basic Techniques: Making Quilts and Pillows. This quilt is made up of two blocks – a Large Cat block (in four different colourways) and a Small Cat block (in six different colourways). Half of the cats face one direction and half in the other direction. The blocks are separated by sashing, vertically and horizontally. The fabrics used are shown in **Fig A**. The quilt layout is shown in **Fig B**, with the various elements identified.

Fig B Quilt layout

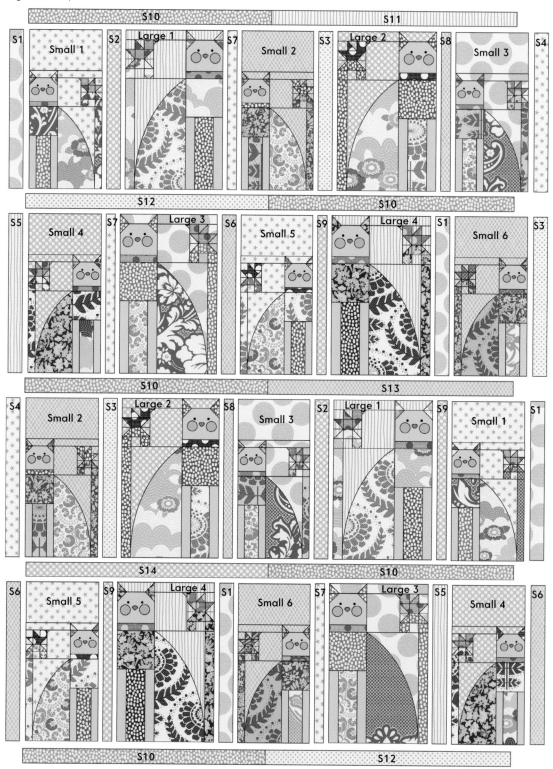

2 The sashing is in two different widths and two different lengths, shown in **Fig C**.

Cut 2in x 17in (5.1cm x 43.2cm) strips for vertical sashing.
• Fabric 8 – four strips.
• Fabric 6 – two strips.
• Fabric 27 – three strips.
• Fabric 17 – two strips.
• Fabric 1 – two strips.
• Fabric 19 – three strips.

Cut 1½in x 17in (3.8cm x 43.2cm) strips for vertical sashing.
• Fabric 17 – three strips.
• Fabric 19 – two strips.
• Fabric 6 – three strips.

Cut 2in x 26¾in (5.1cm x 68cm) strips for horizontal sashing.
• Fabric 28 – five strips.
• Fabric 1 – one strip.
• Fabric 27 – two strips.
• Fabric 19 – one strip.
• Fabric 6 – one strip.

3 Cut the backing fabric in half across the width. Sew the pieces together along the long side. Press the seam open and trim to a piece about 61in x 82in (155cm x 208cm).

4 From the binding fabric cut seven strips 2½in (6.4cm) x width of fabric. Sew together end to end and press the seams open. Press in half along the length, wrong sides together.

5 The cat blocks are made up of many pieces and the sizes to cut are given in diagrams. You may find it easier to cut the pieces and make each block one at a time.

There are eight Large Cat blocks in total, in four different colourways. Each block is made twice – one set facing left and the other set facing right. See **Fig D** for the arrangement of large and small cat blocks. You will see that the layout of the head and legs section is the same for all of the blocks, but the back section is reversed (flipped), to change the direction the cat is facing. **Fig E** shows the layout and cutting for a Large Cat block, so use these measurements when cutting out the fabrics for a block. Measurements include ¼in (6mm) seam allowances.

There are twelve Small Cat blocks in total, in six different colourways. Each block is made twice – one set facing left and the other set facing right. See **Fig F** for the layout and cutting for a Small Cat block.

The fabrics to use are shown in **Fig G** for the Large Cat blocks and **Fig H** for the Small Cat blocks.

Fig C Cutting the sashing

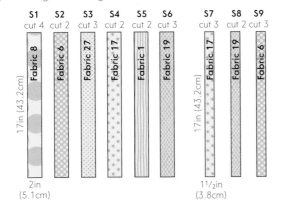

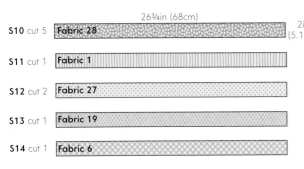

Fig D Cat block arrangements

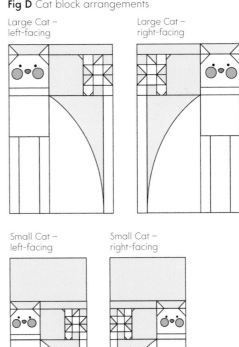

Large Cat – left-facing

Large Cat – right-facing

Small Cat – left-facing

Small Cat – right-facing

Fig E Layout and cutting for the Large Cat blocks

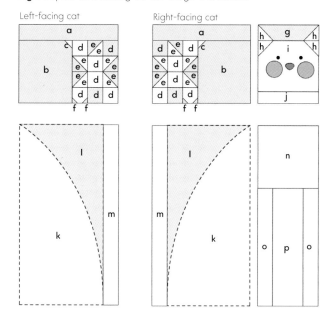

Fig F Layout and cutting for the Small Cat blocks

Bird and Cat Head

a 7in x 1½in (17.8cm x 3.8cm).
b 4in x 4½in (10.2cm x 11.4cm).
c 1in (2.5cm) square.
d 1½in (3.8cm) square.
e 1⅞in (4.8cm) square, for 1½in (3.8cm) unfinished half-square triangle units.
f ⅞in (2.2cm) square.
g 4½in x 1½in (11.4cm x 3.8cm).
h 1½in (3.8cm) square.
i 4½in x 3¾in (11.4cm x 9.5cm).
j 4½in x 1¼in (11.4cm x 3.2cm).

Cat Body

k Use back piece pattern for accurate cutting and piecing.
l Use background piece pattern for accurate cutting and piecing.
m 1½in x 12in (3.8cm x 30.5cm).
n 4½in (11.4cm) square.
o 1½in x 8in (3.8cm x 20.3cm).
p 2½in x 8in (6.4cm x 20.3cm).

Cheeks and nose – use the patterns for the appliqué (see step instructions).
Eyes – stitched with French knots.

Bird and Cat Head

a 5¼in x 1¼in (13.3cm x 3.2cm).
b 3in x 3½in (7.6cm x 9cm).
c ⅞in (2.2cm) square.
d 1¼in (3.2cm) square.
e 1⅝in (4.1cm) square, for 1¼in (3.2cm) unfinished half-square triangle units.
f ¾in (2cm) square.
g 3½in x 1¼in (9cm x 3.2cm).
h 1¼in (3.2cm) square.
i 3½in x 3in (9cm x 7.6cm).
j 3½in x 1in (9cm x 2.5cm).

Cat Body

k Use back piece pattern for accurate cutting and piecing.
l Use background piece pattern for accurate cutting and piecing.
m 1¼in x 9in (3.2cm x 23cm).
n 3½in (9cm) square.
o 1¼in x 6in (3.2cm x 15.2cm).
p 2in x 6in (5.1cm x 15.2cm).
q 8¼in x 4¾in (21cm x 12cm) – top of block.

Cheeks and nose – use the patterns for the appliqué (see step instructions).
Eyes – stitched with French knots.

Fig G Fabrics used for Large Cat blocks
Numbers indicate fabrics used
Make two of each block

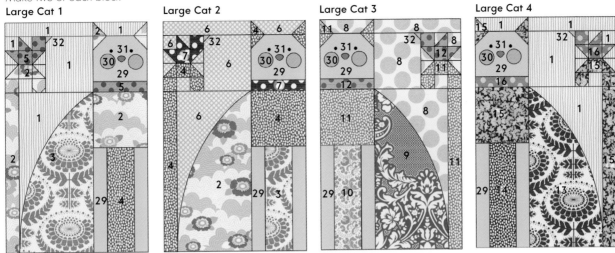

Large Cat 1   Large Cat 2   Large Cat 3   Large Cat 4

Fig H Fabrics used for Small Cat blocks
Numbers indicate fabrics used
Make two of each block

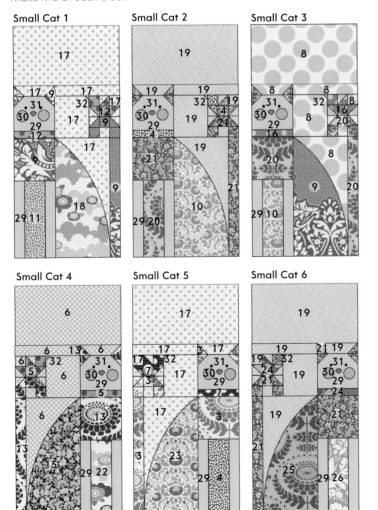

Small Cat 1   Small Cat 2   Small Cat 3

Small Cat 4   Small Cat 5   Small Cat 6

MAKING A LARGE CAT BLOCK

6 Full instructions and diagrams are given here for making Large Cat 1 block. Cut out the pieces needed for the block and roughly arrange the pieces in the block layout. There are only three main techniques needed – making half-square triangle (HST) units, making corner triangle units and making a curved back unit. All of the other pieces are squares and rectangles.

7 Making half-square triangle (HST) units: The bird and the cat's tail need HST units, so make these using a two-at-once method, as follows. For the Large Cat 1 block, take a 1⅞in (4.8cm) square (piece **e**) of Fabric 1 and one of Fabric 5. Pencil mark the diagonal line on the wrong side of one of the squares (**Fig I**). Pin the squares right sides together, with all edges aligned. Sew a *scant* ¼in (6mm) away from the marked line on each side. Cut the units apart on the marked line. Open out each unit and press the seam. Check each HST unit is 1½in (3.8cm) square (unfinished). Repeat to make three HSTs for one bird.

    Make the two HST units for the cat's tail in the same way, using Fabric 1 and Fabric 2.

Fig I Making half-square triangle units

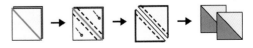

8 Making a corner triangle unit: Some of the points on the patchwork (the bird's beak, the cat's ears and the tip of the tail) are created with small triangles.

For the bird's beak, take one **b** square of Fabric 1 and one **c** square of Fabric 32. Pencil mark the diagonal line on the wrong side of the small square and place it right sides together with the top left corner of the Fabric 1 piece (**Fig J**). Pin if needed and then sew along the marked line as shown and trim off excess fabric ¼in (6mm) outside the sewn line. Press the little triangle outwards.

For the cat's upper ears, take one **g** rectangle of Fabric 1 and two **h** squares of Fabric 2. Using the same technique (shown in second example of **Fig J**), sew the small squares to each side of the rectangle, trim excess and press the triangles downwards.

For the cat's lower ears, take one **i** rectangle of Fabric 29 (the face) and two **h** squares of Fabric 2. Using the same technique, sew the small squares to the top of the rectangle, trim excess and press the triangles upwards.

For the tail tip, take one **d** square of Fabric 2 and two **f** squares of Fabric 1. Using the same technique, sew the small squares to the bottom of the large square, trim excess and press triangles downwards.

9 Making a curved back unit: Use the patterns provided to mark and cut the exact shapes needed (making sure your patterns are full size).

Seam allowances are included on the patterns. For Large Cat 1, cut piece **l** from Fabric 1 and piece **k** from Fabric 3. For cat blocks where the back is curved in the opposite direction, simply reverse (flip) the patterns to cut these shapes.

10 Fold each piece of fabric in half and mark the centre point with a crease or pin (see red marks on **Fig K 1**). Place the pieces right sides together, pinning them together at these centre points (**Fig K 2**). Now ease the rest of the curves together, pinning well to achieve a smooth, curved sewing line. Using a *scant* ¼in (6mm) seam, sew the two pieces together. Snip into the seam at intervals, about ⅛in (3mm) deep and then press the seam outwards. Check the unit is 6in x 12in (15.2cm x 30.5cm) unfinished (**Fig K 3**). (The small cat back unit should be 4½in x 9in (11.4cm x 23cm) once sewn.)

ASSEMBLING A LARGE CAT BLOCK

11 When the pieced units have been made, lay out all of the pieces for a large cat as in **Fig L** (this diagram shows a Large Cat 1 block). Sew the bird and cat face units together first, as in **Fig L 1**, matching up seams neatly where needed and pressing after each stage. Next, sew the back and legs units together (**Fig L 2**). Finally, sew the two parts of the block together (**Fig L 3**). Check the block is 11in x 17in (28cm x 43.2cm).

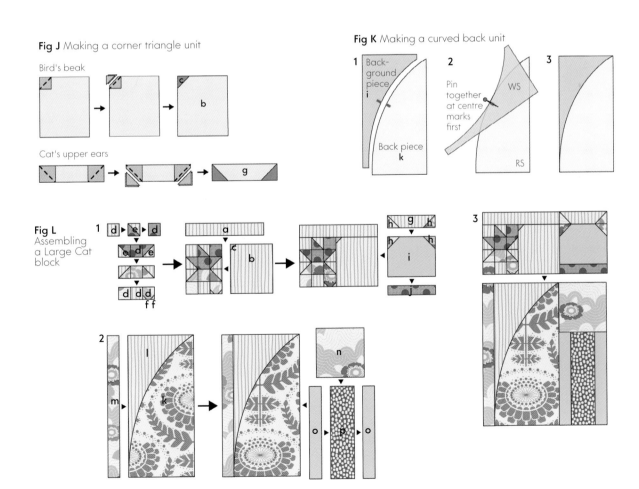

Fig J Making a corner triangle unit

Bird's beak

Cat's upper ears

Fig K Making a curved back unit

1 Background piece **i** — Back piece **k**
2 Pin together at centre marks first — WS — RS
3

Fig L Assembling a Large Cat block

12 Make the rest of the Large Cat blocks in the same way, changing fabrics as indicated in **Fig G**. Remember that half of the blocks need to face in the opposite direction, so follow the diagrams carefully and take care when laying out the pieces and sewing the units together.

MAKING A SMALL CAT BLOCK

13 The small cats are made in the same way as the large cats but using smaller sizes and different fabrics. The Small Cat block also has an extra piece (**q**) at the top of the block, to bring it up to the same height as the larger block. Follow **Fig F** for cutting the pieces and **Fig H** for the fabrics to use.

14 When the pieced units have been made, lay out the block as in **Fig M** (shows a Small Cat 1 block) and sew the pieces together in the same way as the large block. Check the block is 8¼in x 17in (21cm x 43.2cm).

15 Make the rest of the Small Cat blocks in the same way, changing fabrics as indicated in **Fig H**. Remember that half of the blocks need to face in the opposite direction, so take care when laying out the pieces and sewing the units together.

ADDING THE FACE DETAILS

16 Each cat needs two appliqué cheeks. Use the patterns provided (given in large and small cat sizes). Follow the stages of **Fig N** to make an appliqué circle. Cut a 1½in (3.8cm) diameter circle from stiff card and use this to cut two circles from Fabric 30 (**Fig N 1**). Cut the smaller inner circle from stiff card and place this in the centre of

the fabric circle. Use a pencil to mark the circle (**Fig N 2**). Use a doubled thread to sew a circle of gathering stitches about ⅛in (3mm) *outside* of the marked line (**Fig N 3**). Pin the inner card circle back onto the fabric. Pull up the gathering threads, to gather the fabric around the card (**Fig N 4**). Tie off the threads and press well. Remove the card and press again. You can leave the gathering thread in place if it doesn't show. Make all of the cheeks for the large cats like this. For the small cats, use the smaller circle patterns.

17 To make the nose a paper pieced method was used (see **Fig O**). Cut out a piece of Fabric 31 using the outer nose shape pattern – an approximate ⅛in (3mm) seam allowance is given but you can trim this down further if needs be. Snip into the seam allowance at intervals around the shape. Cut the inner shape from paper and lightly glue it in the centre of the wrong side of the fabric shape (**Fig O 1**). Smear a little fabric glue around the edges of the paper pattern and begin to fold and press the fabric edges over onto the paper, forming a smooth curve around the edge of the paper pattern (**Fig O 2**). Continue like this all round the shape. Remove the paper pattern and press firmly (**Fig O 3**). Make all of the noses for the large cats like this. For the small cats, use the smaller nose patterns.

18 Sew the cheeks and nose into place on the cat blocks, using matching thread and tiny stitches. To add the eyes, take a length of black embroidery cotton (floss) and using all six strands, stitch a French knot for each eye, wrapping the thread twice around the needle. You could mark the positions of the eyes first using a pin to wiggle a small hole.

Fig M Assembling a Small Cat block

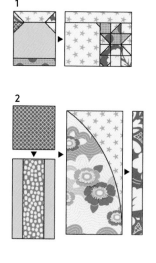
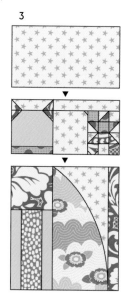

Fig N Making the cheek appliqué

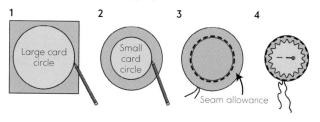

Fig O Making the nose appliqué

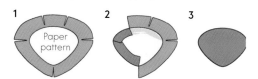

ASSEMBLING THE QUILT

19 Lay out all of the sections of the quilt, following **Fig B** carefully. **Fig P** shows the piecing of the first two rows of the quilt in detail. Begin by sewing the first row of blocks together, with the vertical sashing strips in between using *scant* ¼in (6mm) seams. Note that some of the sashing strips are a narrower width than others, so be sure to put these in the correct places. Press the seams in one direction. Now sew the second row of blocks together, with the vertical sashing strips in between, and press. For each row of horizontal sashing, sew two strips together with a normal ¼in (6mm) seam and press. Sew the horizontal sashing strips above and below the block rows, as shown, and press. Continue in this way to sew the rest of the quilt together, following **Fig B** carefully.

QUILTING AND FINISHING

20 Make a quilt sandwich of the backing fabric, wadding (batting) and quilt. Quilt as desired. Square up the quilt, trimming excess wadding and backing.

21 Use the prepared double-fold binding strip to bind your quilt (see Basic Techniques: Binding). Add a label and your quilt is finished.

Fig P Assembling the first two quilt rows with sashing

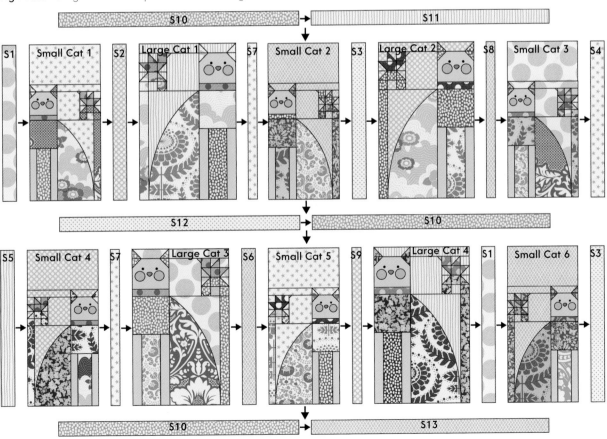

CAT AND BIRD PILLOW

This lovely pillow is the perfect partner to the Cat and Bird Quilt and features two of the cat blocks from the quilt. It uses some of the same fabrics as the quilt, so refer to the fabric swatches in **Fig A** of the quilt instructions. The fabric quantities are much smaller for the pillow. A fat eighth is assumed to be approx. 10½in x 18in (26.7cm x 45.7cm).

MATERIALS
- Fabric 1: fat eighth – Pen Stripe light blue
- Fabric 2: fat eighth – Frances pink
- Fabric 3: 6½in x 12¾in (16.5cm x 32.4cm) – Phoebe ginger
- Fabric 4: 8in (20.3cm) square – Trickles coral
- Fabric 5: 8in (20.3cm) square – Medium Dots salmon
- Fabric 6: 2in x 17in (5.1cm x 43.2cm) – Paint Dots light blue
- Fabric 8: 22¾in x 2in (57.8cm x 5.1cm) – Dottie Dots light blue
- Fabric 10: 5in x 9¾in (12.7cm x 24.8cm) – Mildred lilac
- Fabric 17: 1½in x 17in (3.8cm x 43.2cm) – Tiny Star light blue
- Fabric 19: fat eighth – Crisscross light blue
- Fabric 20: 2in x 6in (5.1cm x 15.2cm) – Phoebe thistle
- Fabric 21: 9in (23cm) square – Josephine emerald
- Fabric 27: 2in x 17in (5.1cm x 43.2cm) – Tiny Dots light blue
- Fabric 28: 22¾in x 2in (57.8cm x 5.1cm) – Trickles teal
- Fabric 29: 12in (30.5cm) square – Solid warm sand
- Fabric 30: scraps – Solid dusty rose
- Fabric 31: scraps – Solid salmon
- Fabric 32: scraps – Solid pale yellow
- Wadding (batting) 24in x 21in (61cm x 53.3cm)
- Lining fabric 24in x 21in (61cm x 53.3cm) (optional)
- Fabric for back of pillow, two pieces 15in x 20in (38cm x 51cm)
- Binding fabric 5in (12.7cm) x width of fabric – Solid lime green
- Black stranded embroidery cotton (floss) for eyes
- Thick card and thick paper for patterns
- Fabric glue for paper piece appliqué
- Pad to fit pillow cover

Finished Size 22¼in x 19½in (56.5cm x 49.5cm)

CUTTING OUT
1 The pillow uses two blocks from the quilt – Large Cat 1 and Small Cat 2 – and these are made in the same way as described for the quilt. Use **Fig E** of the quilt to cut the pieces for a large cat and **Fig F** to cut the pieces for a small cat. The fabrics to use are shown in **Fig G** and **Fig H** of the quilt.

2 The cut sizes of the sashing strips needed are given in the pillow's Materials list here (Fabrics 6, 8, 17, 27 and 28).

3 From the binding fabric cut two strips 2½in (6.4cm) x width of fabric. Sew together into one long length, press the seams open and prepare as a double-fold binding.

MAKING THE PATCHWORK
4 To make the Large Cat 1 block, follow the quilt instructions (Steps 6 to 11).

5 To make the Small Cat 2 block, follow the quilt instructions (Steps 13 and 14).

6 Add the face appliqué and sewing details to both cats, following the quilt instructions (Steps 16 to 18).

7 To assemble the patchwork, lay out the two blocks with the vertical sashing strips between them, as shown in **Fig A** here. Sew the row together and press. Now add the long horizontal sashing strips above and below the patchwork and press. Check the work is 22¾in x 20in (57.8cm x 51cm).

QUILTING AND MAKING UP
8 Make a quilt sandwich of the patchwork, wadding (batting) and lining fabric (if using). Quilt as desired. Trim excess wadding and lining to match the patchwork size.

9 To make up the pillow cover, follow the instructions in Basic Techniques: Bound-Edge Pillow Cover. Insert a pillow pad to finish.

Fig A Assembling the pillow

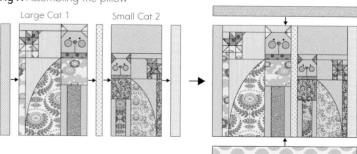

Large Cat 1   Small Cat 2

CROSS QUILT

The patchwork blocks for this lovely quilt are very easy to make, as they are just Nine-Patch blocks. The cross shapes are formed by the blocks in two different colourways. The quilt layout is "on-point", which means the blocks are turned 45 degrees before being sewn together. The quilt uses fabrics from the Bird Pond collection, plus some Medium Dots and some Solid Colour fabrics. The pattern for an alternative blue and ginger colourway is available at www.tildasworld.com. A photo of this quilt is shown later in this chapter.

MATERIALS

- Fabric 1: ¼yd (25cm) – Marnie raspberry
- Fabric 2: ¼yd (25cm) – Tiny Plum pink
- Fabric 3: ¼yd (25cm) – Medium Dots maroon
- Fabric 4: ¼yd (25cm) – Mila lavender
- Fabric 5: ¼yd (25cm) – Solid lavender pink
- Fabric 6: ¼yd (25cm) – Marnie lilac
- Fabric 7: ¼yd (25cm) – Anemone maroon
- Fabric 8: ¼yd (25cm) – Pompom raspberry
- Fabric 9: ¼yd (25cm) – Klara lilac
- Fabric 10: ¼yd (25cm) – Tiny Plum teal
- Fabric 11: ¼yd (25cm) – Elodie honey
- Fabric 12: ¼yd (25cm) – Medium Dots blue
- Fabric 13: ¼yd (25cm) – Medium Dots light grey
- Fabric 14: ¼yd (25cm) – Solid soft teal
- Fabric 15: ¼yd (25cm) – Tiny Plum peach
- Fabric 16: ¼yd (25cm) – Elodie lavender
- Fabric 17: ¼yd (25cm) – Medium Dots teal
- Fabric 18: ¼yd (25cm) – Marnie sand
- Fabric 19: 1⅜yd (1.25m) – Solid dove white
- Backing fabric 3⅜yds (3.1m)
- Wadding (batting) 60in x 76in (152.5cm x 193cm)
- Binding fabric ½yd (50cm) – Medium Dots ginger

Finished Size 51in x 68in (129.5cm x 172.7cm)

Fig A Fabric swatches – if you can't source a fabric, replace with one in a similar colour

Fabric 1
Marnie raspberry

Fabric 8
Pompom raspberry

Fabric 15
Tiny Plum peach

Fabric 2
Tiny Plum pink

Fabric 9
Klara lilac

Fabric 16
Elodie lavender

Fabric 3
Medium Dots maroon

Fabric 10
Tiny Plum teal

Fabric 17
Medium Dots teal

Fabric 4
Mila lavender pink

Fabric 11
Elodie honey

Fabric 18
Marnie sand

Fabric 5
Solid lavender pink

Fabric 12
Medium Dots blue

Fabric 19
Solid dove white

Fabric 6
Marnie lilac

Fabric 13
Medium Dots light grey

Fabric 7
Anemone maroon

Fabric 14
Solid soft teal

PREPARATION AND CUTTING OUT

1 Before you start, refer to Basic Techniques: Making Quilts and Pillows. The quilt is made up of sixty easy Nine-Patch blocks – thirty in one colourway and thirty in a second colourway. See **Fig A** for the fabrics used. The pieced blocks are laid out on point, in cross patterns, with Solid dove white squares in between. Triangles of solid fabric fill in at the sides of the quilt. See **Fig B** for the quilt layout.

2 For the Nine-Patch blocks, from Fabrics 1 to 18, cut two strips 2½in (6.4cm) x width of fabric from each fabric. Cut these strips into 2½in (6.4cm) squares. You will need thirty squares from each fabric (540 squares in total).

Fig B The quilt layout

3 From Fabric 19 cut the following.

• Twenty-three 6½in (16.5cm) squares, for the plain blocks.

• Six 9¾in (24.8cm) squares. Cut each square along both diagonals to make four triangles from each square (for a total of twenty-four setting triangles).

• Two squares 5¼in (13.3cm). Cut each square once along one diagonal (for a total of four corner triangles).

4 Cut the backing fabric across the width into two pieces. Using a ¼in (6mm) seam, sew together along the long side and press the seam open. Trim to a piece about 60in x 76in (152.5cm x 193cm).

5 Cut the binding fabric into seven strips 2½in (6.4cm) x width of fabric. Sew the strips together end to end and press seams open. Press in half along the length, wrong sides together.

MAKING THE NINE-PATCH BLOCKS

6 There are two different colours of these blocks. Block 1 is mostly red fabrics (Fabrics 1 to 9) and thirty of these blocks are needed. Block 2 is mostly teals (Fabrics 10 to 18) and thirty are needed.

7 To make Block 1 follow **Fig C**, laying out nine squares in the fabrics shown. Using a ¼in (6mm) seam, sew the squares together in rows and press. Now sew the rows together, matching seams neatly and press. Check the block is 6½in (16.5cm) square. Repeat to make thirty blocks in total.

8 To make Block 2 follow **Fig D**, making the block in the same way as Block 1. Repeat to make thirty blocks in total.

Fig C Making Block 1
Numbers show fabrics used

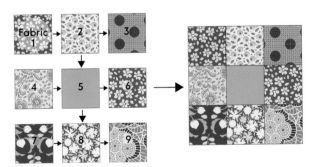

Fig D Making Block 2
Numbers show fabrics used

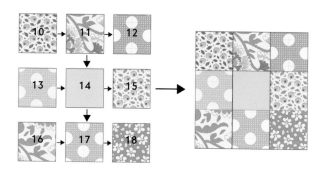

ASSEMBLING THE QUILT

9 The blocks need to be sewn together in a diagonal way. Lay out the Nine-Patch blocks, the plain blocks and the large triangles in the order shown in the quilt layout in **Fig B**. You will notice that the blocks are in a repeating cross pattern.

10 When sewing the side setting triangles to the blocks you will need to use an offset seam, as shown in **Fig E**. This will ensure that the triangle and square line up well once sewn together. Sew the blocks together in diagonal rows, starting with Row 1 and then Row 2, Row 3 and so on. **Fig F** shows the first six rows. Press the seams of alternate rows in opposite directions.

11 Once all the rows are sewn, sew them together, matching seams neatly, and then press. Finally, add the four smaller triangles, one to each corner (**Fig G**).

QUILTING AND FINISHING

12 Make a quilt sandwich of the backing fabric, wadding (batting) and quilt top. Quilt as desired. Square up the quilt, trimming excess wadding and backing.

13 Use the prepared double-fold binding strip to bind your quilt (see Basic Techniques: Binding). Add a label and your quilt is finished.

Fig E Adding a setting triangle to a block

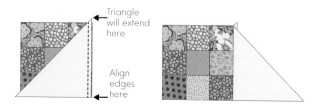

Fig F Sewing the diagonal rows

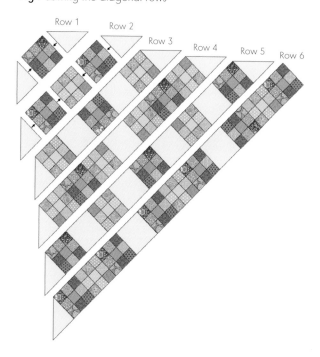

Fig G Adding the corner triangles

PLAID QUILT

The patchwork for this quilt is easier to make than it looks as the chequered pattern is created by different rows of repeating fabrics. The fabrics are from the Bird Pond collection, plus some Medium Dots and three Solid Colours.

MATERIALS

- Fabric 1: ⅜yd (40cm) – Anemone night blue
- Fabric 2: ⅜yd (40cm) – Tiny Plum teal
- Fabric 3: ⅜yd (40cm) – Mila lavender
- Fabric 4: ⅜yd (40cm) – Lovebirds ginger
- Fabric 5: ⅜yd (40cm) – Medium Dots blue
- Fabric 6: ⅜yd (40cm) – Pompom blue
- Fabric 7: ½yd (50cm) – Elodie lavender
- Fabric 8: ½yd (50cm) – Marnie night blue
- Fabric 9: ½yd (50cm) – Solid warm sand
- Fabric 10: 1yd (1m) – Solid dove white
- Fabric 11: ½yd (50cm) – Solid soft teal
- Backing fabric 3⅜yds (3.1m)
- Wadding (batting) 60in x 85in (152.5cm x 216cm)
- Binding fabric ½yd (50cm) – Medium Dots ginger

Finished Size 51in x 76¼in (129.5cm x 193.7cm)

Fig A Fabric swatches – if you can't source a fabric, replace with one in a similar colour

Fabric 1
Anemone
night blue

Fabric 7
Elodie
lavender

Fabric 2
Tiny Plum
teal

Fabric 8
Marnie
night blue

Fabric 3
Mila
lavender

Fabric 9
Solid
warm sand

Fabric 4
Lovebirds
ginger

Fabric 10
Solid
dove white

Fabric 5
Medium Dots
blue

Fabric 11
Solid
soft teal

Fabric 6
Pompom
blue

PREPARATION AND CUTTING OUT

1 Before you start, refer to Basic Techniques: Making Quilts and Pillows. The quilt is made up of thirty-one rows of alternating squares and rectangles in repeating fabric patterns, which create a plaid effect when seen on-point. See **Fig A** for the fabrics used and **Fig B** for the quilt layout.

Fig B Quilt layout

2 The quilt is made up of 2½in (6.4cm) squares in Fabrics 1 to 6 and 2½in x 4½in (6.4cm x 11.4cm) rectangles in Fabrics 7 to 11. To cut out the pieces, follow **Fig C**, which gives the numbers of each shape to cut (seam allowances are included). It is best to cut 2½in (6.4cm) strips across the fabric width and then sub-cut the strips into individual squares and rectangles.

3 Cut the backing fabric across the width into two pieces. Using a ¼in (6mm) seam, sew together along the long side and press the seam open. Trim to a piece about 60in x 85in (152.5cm x 216cm).

4 Cut the binding fabric into seven strips 2½in (6.4cm) x width of fabric. Sew the strips together end to end and press seams open. Press in half along the length, wrong sides together.

PIECING THE QUILT ROWS

5 The squares and rectangles are sewn together in a repeating pattern. **Figs D** and **E** show the patterns, which you can follow if you wish to make smaller sections first. **Fig F** shows all the rows of the quilt, so you could just work from this diagram if you prefer.

Fig C Cutting out

Cut 2½in (6.4cm) squares

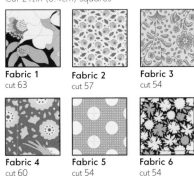

Fabric 1
cut 63

Fabric 2
cut 57

Fabric 3
cut 54

Fabric 4
cut 60

Fabric 5
cut 54

Fabric 6
cut 54

Cut 2½in x 4½in (6.4cm x 11.4cm) rectangles

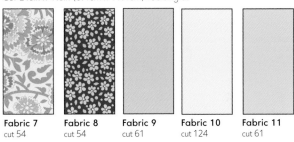

Fabric 7
cut 54

Fabric 8
cut 54

Fabric 9
cut 61

Fabric 10
cut 124

Fabric 11
cut 61

Fig D Rectangles order

Rectangle row – order A, repeated along row

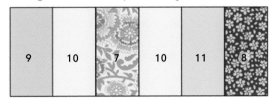

| 9 | 10 | 7 | 10 | 11 | 8 |

Rectangle row – order B, repeated along alternate rows

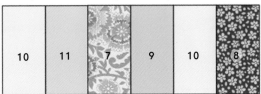

| 10 | 11 | 7 | 9 | 10 | 8 |

Fig E Squares order

Square row – order A   Square row – order B

1 2 3 4 5 6   1 3 2 4 6 5

Alternate order A and order B along a row

6 When the individual rows are sewn, lay out the thirty-one rows, making sure you place them in the correct order (see **Fig F**). Note that the rows step down from Row 1. Sew the pieces of each row together. Press odd rows in one direction and even rows in the opposite direction. Now sew the rows together, matching seams neatly and press.

7 When the quilt is fully assembled, press it once more. Now lay the quilt flat on the biggest cutting mat you have and use a large quilting ruler (one 24in long if you have it) to trim off excess fabric around the edges (see **Fig G**). You will need to move the quilt frequently to trim all round. Make sure the corners are cut at right angles.

QUILTING AND FINISHING

8 Make a quilt sandwich of the backing fabric, wadding (batting) and quilt top. Quilt as desired. Square up the quilt, trimming excess wadding and backing.

9 Use your prepared double-fold binding strip to bind your quilt (see Basic Techniques: Binding). Add a label and your quilt is finished.

Fig F Piecing the quilt rows

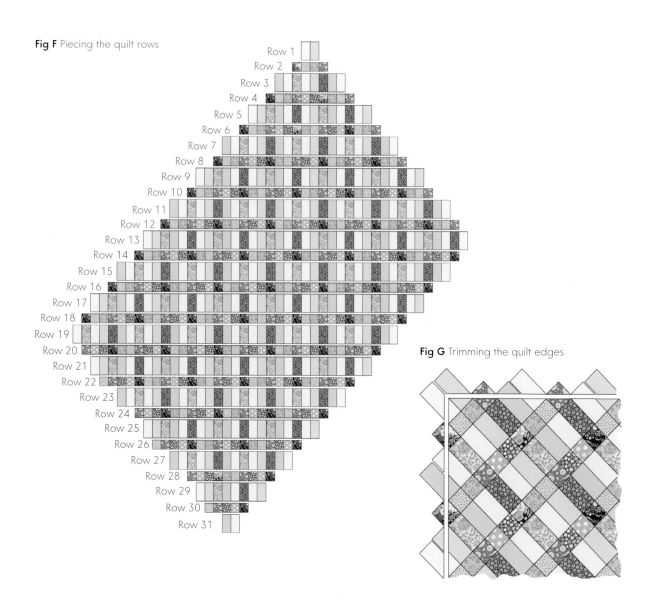

Fig G Trimming the quilt edges

DUCK QUILT

Two patchwork blocks are used for this pretty quilt – a star block and a duck block, which create an interesting diagonal pattern over the quilt. The duck block is made in two variations, so one duck faces right and one left. The quilt uses fabrics from the Bird Pond collection, plus some Medium Dots and Solid Colour fabrics.

MATERIALS

- Fabric 1: 4yd (3.7m) – Medium Dots light grey
- Fabric 2: ⅛yd (15cm) – Marnie honey
- Fabric 3: ⅛yd (15cm) – Klara ginger
- Fabric 4: ⅛yd (15cm) – Tiny Plum teal
- Fabric 5: ¼yd (25cm) – Elodie lavender
- Fabric 6: ¼yd (25cm) – Marnie night blue
- Fabric 7: ¼yd (25cm) – Pompom blue
- Fabric 8: ⅜yd (40cm) – Solid lilac mist
- Fabric 9: ⅜yd (40cm) – Solid thistle
- Fabric 10: ¼yd (25cm) – Anemone night blue
- Fabric 11: ¼yd (25cm) – Elodie lilac blue
- Fabric 12: ¼yd (25cm) – Mila lavender
- Fabric 13: ¼yd (25cm) – Klara lilac
- Fabric 14: ¼yd (25cm) – Pompom raspberry
- Fabric 15: ¼yd (25cm) – Anemone maroon
- Fabric 16: ¼yd (25cm) – Marnie lilac
- Fabric 17: ¼yd (25cm) – Elodie honey
- Fabric 18: ¼yd (25cm) – Marnie sand
- Fabric 19: 1⅜yd (1.25m) – Lovebirds ginger
- Fabric 20: ¼yd (25cm) – Tiny Plum peach
- Fabric 21: ¼yd (25cm) – Anemone sand
- Backing fabric 3¾yds (3.4m)
- Wadding (batting) 64in x 80in (162.5cm x 203cm)
- Binding fabric ½yd (50cm) – Medium Dots maroon

Finished Size 56in x 72in (142.2cm x 183cm)

Fig A Fabric swatches – if you can't source a fabric, replace with one in a similar colour

Fabric 1
Medium Dots light grey

Fabric 8
Solid lilac mist

Fabric 15
Anemone maroon

Fabric 2
Marnie honey

Fabric 9
Solid thistle

Fabric 16
Marnie lilac

Fabric 3
Klara ginger

Fabric 10
Anemone night blue

Fabric 17
Elodie honey

Fabric 4
Tiny Plum teal

Fabric 11
Elodie lilac blue

Fabric 18
Marine sand

Fabric 5
Elodie lavender

Fabric 12
Mila lavender

Fabric 19
Lovebirds ginger

Fabric 6
Marnie night blue

Fabric 13
Klara lilac

Fabric 20
Tiny Plum peach

Fabric 7
Pompom blue

Fabric 14
Pompom raspberry

Fabric 21
Anemone sand

PREPARATION AND CUTTING OUT

1 Before you start, refer to Basic Techniques: Making Quilts and Pillows. The quilt is made up of sixty-three blocks in a 7 x 9 block layout – thirty-two Star blocks, sixteen Right Duck blocks and fifteen Left Duck blocks. See **Fig A** for the fabrics used and **Fig B** for the quilt layout.

Fig B Quilt layout

2 For one Star block cut the following pieces (see **Fig C** for the measurements and **Fig D** for the fabrics used).

- From Fabric 1 cut four 2½in (6.4cm) squares.
- From Fabric 1 cut four 4½in x 2½in (11.4cm x 6.4cm) rectangles (for flying geese units).
- From Fabrics 10, 11, 12, 13, 14, 15, 16 and 17, cut one 2½in (6.4cm) square (for flying geese units).
- From Fabric 1 cut four 2⅞in (7.3cm) squares (for half-square triangle units). Note, this will make enough half-square triangle (HST) units for two blocks.
- From Fabrics 18, 19, 20 and 21, cut one 2⅞in (7.3cm) square (for HSTs).

3 For one Right Duck block cut the following pieces (see **Fig E** for the measurements and **Fig F** for the fabrics used).

- From Fabric 1 cut two 8½in x 2½in (21.6cm x 6.4cm) rectangles.
- From Fabric 9 cut four 2½in (6.4cm) squares.
- From Fabric 1 cut two 2⅞in (7.3cm) squares (for HSTs).
- From Fabric 6 and Fabric 7 cut one 2⅞in (7.3cm) square (for HSTs).
- From Fabric 1 and Fabric 5 cut one 3in x 2½in (7.6cm x 6.4cm) rectangle.
- From Fabric 1 cut one 2¾in x 4½in (7cm x 11.4cm) rectangle.
- From Fabric 2 cut one 1¼in (3.2cm) square.
- From Fabric 3 and Fabric 4 cut one 1¾in x 2½in (4.4cm x 6.4cm) rectangle.

Fig C Star block measurements
Measurements are cut sizes (or unfinished sizes)

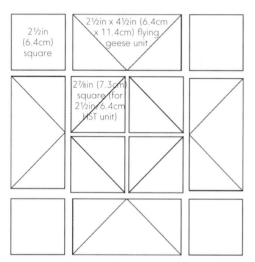

Fig E Right Duck block measurements
Measurements are cut sizes (or unfinished sizes)

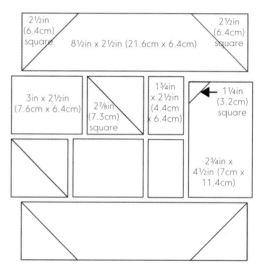

Fig D Fabrics for a Star block
Numbers show fabrics used

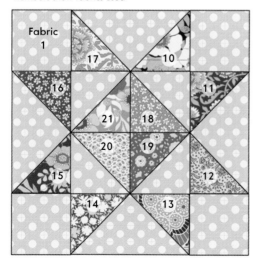

Fig F Fabrics for a Right Duck block

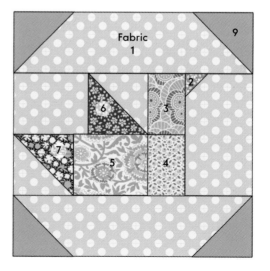

4 For one Left Duck block cut out the same pieces as the Right Duck block but change the four 2½in (6.4cm) squares of Fabric 9 (Solid thistle) to Fabric 8 (Solid lilac mist). See **Fig G** for the measurements and **Fig H** for the fabrics used.

5 Cut the backing fabric across the width into two pieces. Using a ¼in (6mm) seam, sew together along the long side and press the seam open. Trim to a piece about 64in x 80in (162.5cm x 203cm).

6 Cut the binding fabric into seven strips 2½in (6.4cm) x width of fabric. Sew the strips together end to end and press seams open. Press in half along the length, wrong sides together.

Fig G Left Duck block measurements
Measurements are cut sizes (or unfinished sizes)

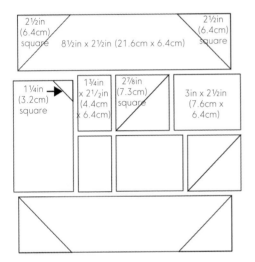

Fig H Fabrics for a Left Duck block

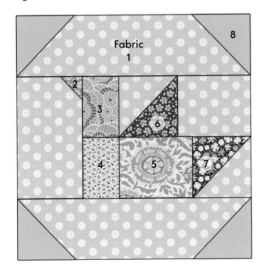

MAKING THE STAR BLOCKS

7 The Star blocks use half-square triangle (HST) units. **Fig I** shows how to make these using a two-at-once method. (Note that the diagram is shown in shades of grey.) Take one 2⅞in (7.3cm) square of Fabric 1 and one of Fabric 18 and place them right sides together. Mark the diagonal line and sew a scant ¼in (6mm) away from the line on both sides. Cut the units apart and press them. The units should be 2½in (6.4cm) square. The method makes two units, so save one for another block. Repeat this to make HSTs from Fabrics 1 and 19, Fabrics 1 and 20 and Fabrics 1 and 21 (see **Fig D**).

8 The Star blocks also need flying geese units. **Fig J** shows how to make one of these units. Note that the flying geese use two different print fabrics for the corner triangles. Take one Fabric 1 rectangle 4½in x 2½in (11.4cm x 6.4cm), one Fabric 17 square 2½in

(6.4cm) and one Fabric 10 square 2½in (6.4cm). Mark a diagonal line on the back of both squares. Put the Fabric 17 square right sides together with the rectangle and sew along the diagonal line. (Note that the diagram is shown in shades of grey.) Trim the excess and press the triangle outwards. Repeat with a Fabric 10 square on the other end of the rectangle. The unit should be 4½in x 2½in (11.4cm x 6.4cm). Repeat this to make flying geese from Fabrics 1, 11 and 12, Fabrics 1, 13 and 14 and Fabrics 1, 15 and 16 (see **Fig D**).

9 To assemble the block lay out four HSTs for the block centre, four flying geese units and four squares of Fabric 1, as in **Fig K**. Sew the units together into rows and press. Sew the rows together, matching seams neatly, and press. Check the block is 8½in (21.6cm) square. Repeat to make thirty-two blocks in total.

Fig I Making half-square triangle units

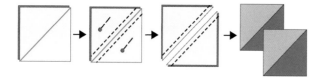

Fig J Making flying geese units

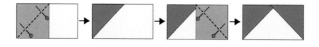

Fig K Making a Star block

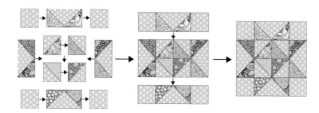

Fig L Making the units of a Right Duck block

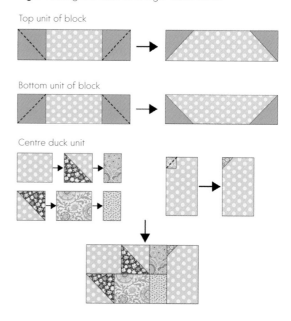

MAKING THE DUCK BLOCKS

10 There are thirty-one of these blocks – sixteen with ducks facing right and fifteen facing left. The instructions are for a Right Duck block. The Left Duck block is made the same way, with the same pieces but with the block assembled as a reversed (flipped) version.

11 Take all of the pieces for one Right Duck block as in **Fig F**. Follow **Fig L** to sew the various units of the block. To create a triangle on the corner of the top and bottom units of the block, place a square of Fabric 9 right side down on an 8½in x 2½in (21.6cm x 6.4cm) rectangle of Fabric 1. Mark the diagonal and then sew as shown. Trim excess fabric and press the triangle outwards. Repeat on the other end of the rectangle. Repeat this process to sew the bottom unit.

12 Make the HSTs for the block using the method previously described. Follow **Fig L** to sew the duck together. Now sew the block's units together (**Fig M**). Check the block is 8½in (21.6cm) square. Repeat to make sixteen of these blocks in total.

13 Repeat the same process to make fifteen Left Duck blocks, arranging the units as in **Fig H**, so the duck faces left.

ASSEMBLING THE QUILT

14 Follow the quilt layout in **Fig B** to sew the blocks together into nine rows, alternating Star blocks and Duck blocks within each row. Place Left Ducks in Row 1, Right Ducks in Row 2, and so on. **Fig N** shows the first two rows assembled. Once all the rows are sewn, sew them together, matching seams neatly, and then press.

QUILTING AND FINISHING

15 Make a quilt sandwich of the backing fabric, wadding (batting) and quilt top. Quilt as desired. Square up the quilt, trimming excess wadding and backing.

16 Use the prepared double-fold binding strip to bind your quilt (see Basic Techniques: Binding). Add a label and your quilt is finished.

Fig M Assembling a Right Duck block

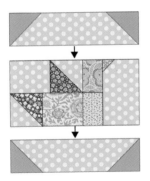

Fig N Assembling the quilt rows

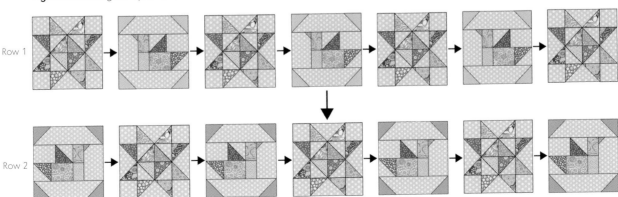

Row 1

Row 2

PLUM PARTY QUILT

You are sure to have a fun time making this gorgeous quilt. It looks complicated but most of the pattern is built up from simple patchwork units. The curved shapes for the angel's dress are achieved by using the patterns provided.

MATERIALS

- Fabric 1: 4½yd (4.1m) – Solid lupine
- Fabric 2: ¼yd (25cm) – Solid warm sand
- Fabric 3: ¼yd (25cm) – Solid blue sage
- Fabric 4: 7in (18cm) square – Solid dusty rose
- Fabric 5: ¼yd (25cm) – Teardrop peach
- Fabric 6: ¼yd (25cm) – Teardrop blueberry
- Fabric 7: ¼yd (25cm) – Teardrop plum
- Fabric 8: ¼yd (25cm) – Autumn Bouquet peach
- Fabric 9: 7in (18cm) square – Autumn Bouquet blue
- Fabric 10: 12in (30.5cm) square – Autumn Bouquet teal
- Fabric 11: ¼yd (25cm) – Autumn Bouquet lavender
- Fabric 12: ¼yd (25cm) – Duck Nest peach
- Fabric 13: ¼yd (25cm) – Duck Nest blueberry
- Fabric 14: ¼yd (25cm) – Duck Nest plum
- Fabric 15: ¼yd (25cm) – Flower Confetti sand
- Fabric 16: ⅜yd (40cm) – Flower Confetti blue
- Fabric 17: ⅛yd (15cm) – Flower Confetti plum
- Fabric 18: 7in (18cm) square – Windflower red
- Fabric 19: ¼yd (25cm) – Windflower blueberry
- Fabric 20: ¼yd (25cm) – Windflower lavender
- Fabric 21: ⅛yd (15cm) – Berry Jam teal
- Fabric 22: ⅛yd (15cm) – Berry Jam plum
- Fabric 23: ⅛yd (15cm) – Berry Jam peach
- Fabric 24: ⅛yd (15cm) – Berry Jam blue
- Fabric 25: ¼yd (25cm) – Berry Jam wicker
- Fabric 26: 7in (18cm) square – Biscuit Stripe blue
- Fabric 27: 12in (30.5cm) square – Cookie Stripe blue
- Fabric 28: 12in (30.5cm) square – Scone Stripe teal
- Fabric 29: 7in (18cm) square – Spongecake Stripe teal
- Fabric 30: 12in (30.5cm) square – Brownie Stripe plum
- Fabric 31: 7in (18cm) square – Cantucci Stripe plum
- Backing fabric 5⅛yd (4.7m)
- Wadding (batting) 69in x 91in (175cm x 231cm)
- Binding fabric ⅝yd (60cm) – Cookie Stripe blue
- Erasable marker
- Thick card circles for appliqué (see patterns)

Finished Size 61in x 83in (155cm x 211cm)

Fig A Fabric swatches – if you can't source a fabric, replace with one in a similar colour

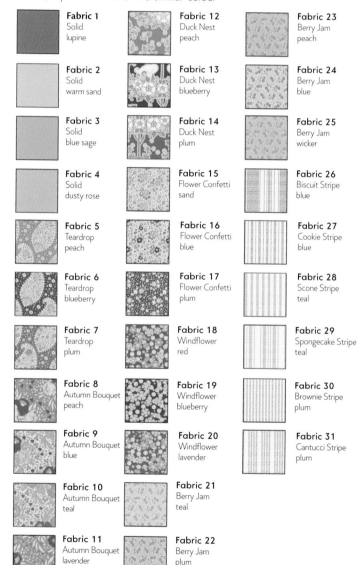

Fabric 1 Solid lupine
Fabric 2 Solid warm sand
Fabric 3 Solid blue sage
Fabric 4 Solid dusty rose
Fabric 5 Teardrop peach
Fabric 6 Teardrop blueberry
Fabric 7 Teardrop plum
Fabric 8 Autumn Bouquet peach
Fabric 9 Autumn Bouquet blue
Fabric 10 Autumn Bouquet teal
Fabric 11 Autumn Bouquet lavender
Fabric 12 Duck Nest peach
Fabric 13 Duck Nest blueberry
Fabric 14 Duck Nest plum
Fabric 15 Flower Confetti sand
Fabric 16 Flower Confetti blue
Fabric 17 Flower Confetti plum
Fabric 18 Windflower red
Fabric 19 Windflower blueberry
Fabric 20 Windflower lavender
Fabric 21 Berry Jam teal
Fabric 22 Berry Jam plum
Fabric 23 Berry Jam peach
Fabric 24 Berry Jam blue
Fabric 25 Berry Jam wicker
Fabric 26 Biscuit Stripe blue
Fabric 27 Cookie Stripe blue
Fabric 28 Scone Stripe teal
Fabric 29 Spongecake Stripe teal
Fabric 30 Brownie Stripe plum
Fabric 31 Cantucci Stripe plum

Fabric Note Where a long eighth or long quarter of a yard is given in the Materials list you could use fat eighths and fat quarters instead. A fat eighth is assumed to be approximately 10½in x 18in (26.7cm x 45.7cm) and a fat quarter approximately 21in x 18in (53.3cm x 45.7cm).

PREPARATION AND CUTTING OUT

1 Before you start, refer to Basic Techniques: Making Quilts and Pillows. This quilt is made up of two large blocks – a Fruit Bowl block (in three different colourways) and an Angel block (in three different colourways). These blocks are separated by columns of pieced sashing, using plum and pinwheel units, and two horizontal pieced flag borders. The fabrics used are shown in **Fig A**. The quilt layout is shown in **Fig B**, with the various elements identified by capital letters.

2 The Fruit Bowl and Angel blocks are made up of many pieces, so the layout and sizes to cut are given in diagrams. You will probably find it easier to cut the pieces and make each block one at a time.

3 The cut sizes for the sashing sections and the horizontal borders are given in diagrams and in the making instructions.

4 Cut the backing fabric in half across the width. Sew the pieces together along the long side. Press the seam open and trim to a piece about 69in x 91in (175cm x 231cm).

5 From the binding fabric cut eight strips 2½in (6.4cm) x width of fabric. Sew together end to end and press the seams open. Press in half along the length, wrong sides together.

MAKING A FRUIT BOWL BLOCK

6 There are three of these blocks in the quilt – see A1, A2 and A3 on **Fig B**. All of the blocks are made the same way but with different fabrics. The instructions here will describe and illustrate Fruit Bowl block 1. The block is made up of three 'tiers' – a bird unit, a plums unit and a bowl unit. **Fig C** shows the fabrics used for each of the blocks. Follow **Fig D** carefully to cut out the pieces for one block (measurements include ¼in/6mm seam allowances). Arrange the cut pieces roughly in the block layout.

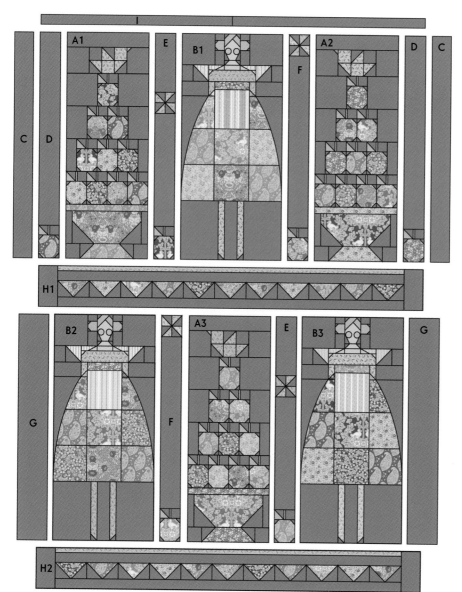

Fig B Quilt layout
A Fruit Bowl blocks 1, 2 & 3
B Angel blocks 1, 2 & 3
C Sashing 1
D Sashing 2
E Sashing 3
F Sashing 4
G Sashing 5
H Flag borders 1 & 2
I Top border

Fig C Fabrics used for Fruit Bowl blocks
Numbers indicate fabrics used

Fruit Bowl 1 **Fruit Bowl 2** **Fruit Bowl 3**

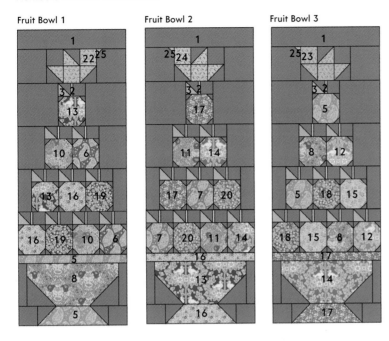

Fig D Layout and cutting for a Fruit Bowl block

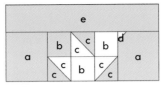

Bird
a 4in x 4½in (10.2cm x 11.4cm).
b 2½in (6.4cm) square.
c 2⅞in (7.3cm) square to make
   2½in (6.4cm) half-square triangle
   (HST) units.
d 1¼in (3.2cm) square.
e 13½in x 2¾in (34.3cm x 7cm).

Single plum
a 2⅜in (6cm) square, to make 2in
   (5.1cm) half-square triangles.
b ¾in x 2in (2cm x 5.1cm).
c 2in (5.1cm) square.
d 3¾in x 4in (9.5cm x 10.2cm).
e 1¼in (3.2cm) square.

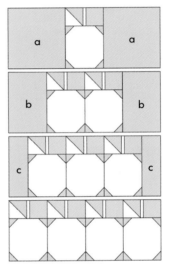

Plum rows filler pieces
a 5⅜in x 5½in (13.6cm x 14cm).
b 3¾in x 5½in (9.5cm x 14cm).
c 2⅛in x 5½in (5.4cm x 14cm).

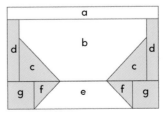

Bowl
a 13½in x 1½in (34.3cm x 3.8cm).
b 11½in x 5½in (29.2cm x 14cm).
c 4in (10.2cm) square.
d 1½in x 5½in (3.8cm x 14cm).
e 9in x 2¾in (22.9cm x 7cm).
f 2¾in (7cm) square.
g 2¾in (7cm) square.

7 Making a bird unit: This unit uses half-square triangle (HST) units, so make these first, using a two-at-once method, as described in Basic Techniques: Half-Square Triangle Units. For Block A1, use a 2⅞in (7.3cm) square (piece **c**) of Fabric 1 and one of Fabric 22. Check each sewn HST unit is 2½in (6.4cm) square (unfinished). Repeat to make three HSTs for one bird unit.

8 The little beak on the bird is created by making a corner triangle, as described in Basic Techniques: Corner Square Unit. For Block A1 use piece **d** of Fabric 25 and piece **a** of Fabric 1.

9 Take all of the pieces for the bird unit and sew them together following the stages shown in **Fig E**. Press the unit.

Fig E Assembling a bird unit

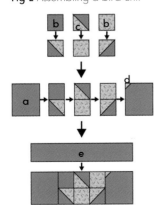

10 Making a single plum unit: This unit is used in the Fruit Bowl blocks and also in most of the sashing units. The plums are all made with the same sizes of cut pieces, but the fabrics for the plum itself vary. Fruit Bowl block 1 is described here. Make one plum unit as follows. Take a 2⅜in (6cm) **a** square of Fabric 1 and one of Fabric 3 and make HST units, as described in Step 7 above. This time, each HST unit should be 2in (5.1cm) square (unfinished). Reserve the spare unit for another plum later.

11 Create the body of the plum using piece **d** of Fabric 13 and four **e** pieces of Fabric 1. Create a corner triangle on each of the four corners using the method described in Basic Techniques: Corner Square Unit. Now sew the plum together as in **Fig F**. A single plum should be 3¾in x 5½in (9.5cm x 14cm) at this stage. Make another

nine plums, using the fabrics shown in **Fig C** for Fruit Bowl 1. Assemble the plum rows as in **Fig G**, using filler pieces **a**, **b** and **c** in the positions shown.

12 Making a bowl unit: For Fruit Bowl 1, see **Fig D** for the cut pieces and **Fig H** for the assembly. Take the **b** piece and two **c** pieces and create corner triangles, as before. Take the **e** piece and the **f** pieces and create corner triangles, as before. Sew pieces **d** to **b/c** and sew pieces **g** to **e/f** as shown. Now join the three sections of the bowl together and press.

13 To assemble the Fruit Bowl block, take the bird unit, plums unit and bowl unit, sew them together and press. The block should be 13½in x 35in (34.3cm x 89cm) at this stage.

Fig F Assembling a single plum unit

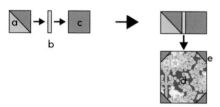

Fig G Assembling the plum rows

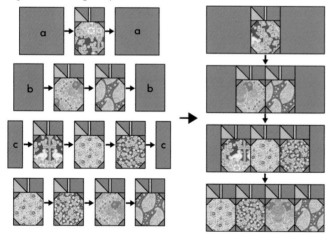

Fig H Assembling the bowl unit

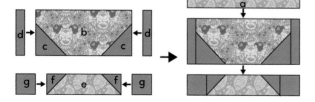

Fig I Fabrics used for Angel blocks

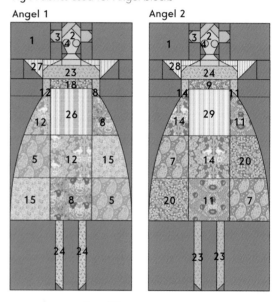

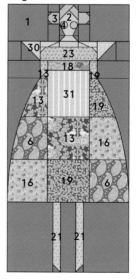

Fig J Layout and cutting for an Angel block

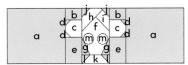

Head
a 5¾in x 5¼in (14.6cm x 13.3cm).
b 2in x 1½in (5.1cm x 3.8cm).
c 2in (5.1cm) square.
d 1in (2.5cm) square.
e 2in x 2¾in (5.1cm x 7cm).
f 3in x 4½in (7.6cm x 11.4cm).
g 1¼in x 2in (3.2cm x 5.1cm).
h 2½in (6.4cm) square.
i 2½in (6.4cm) square.
j 1¼in (3.2cm) square.
k 3in x 1¼in (7.6cm x 3.2cm).
l 1¼in (3.2cm) square.
m 1½in (3.8cm) diameter.

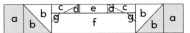

Shoulders and wings
a 2¼in x 3in (5.7cm x 7.6cm).
b 3⅜in (8.6cm) square, for 3in (7.6cm) HST (unfinished).
c 3in x 1¼in (7.6cm x 3.2cm).
d 2in x 1¼in (5.1cm x 3.2cm).
e 3in x 1¼in (7.6cm x 3.2cm).
f 8in x 2¼in (20.3cm x 5.7cm).
g 1¼in (3.2cm) square.

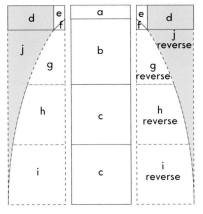

Dress
a 6in x 1¾in (15.2cm x 4.4cm).
b 6in x 6½in (15.2cm x 16.5cm).
c 6in (15.2cm) square.
d 4¾in x 2¾in (12cm x 7cm).
e 1½in x 2¾in (3.8cm x 7cm).
f 1½in (3.8cm) square.

Cut pieces **g**, **h**, **i** and **j** using the full-size patterns.

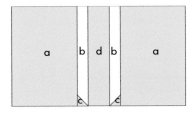

Legs
a 6½in x 9½in (16.5cm x 24.1cm).
b 1½in x 9½in (3.8cm x 24.1cm).
c 1½in (3.8cm) square.
d 2½in x 9½in (6.4cm x 24.1cm).

14 Repeat this whole process to make a Fruit Bowl 2 block and then a Fruit Bowl 3 block, following the fabric positions in **Fig C**.

MAKING AN ANGEL BLOCK
15 There are three of these blocks in the quilt – see B1, B2 and B3 on **Fig B**. All of the blocks are made the same way but with different fabrics. The instructions here will describe and illustrate Angel block 1. The block is made up of four sections – a head unit, shoulders and wings unit, dress unit and legs unit. **Fig I** shows the fabrics used for each of the blocks. Follow **Fig J** carefully to cut out the pieces for one block (measurements include ¼in (6mm) seam allowances). Arrange the cut pieces roughly in the block layout. The shaping of the curved dress pieces will be described later.

16 Making the head unit: Start by making the hair buns, using a **c** piece of Fabric 3 and two **d** pieces of Fabric 1. Create corner triangles on the left-hand side of the larger square, using the same method as before. Sew a **b** piece of Fabric 1 to the top of this **c/d** unit and an **e** piece of Fabric 1 to the bottom (**Fig K**). Repeat this process to make another **a/b/c/d** unit but this time with the bun facing the other way. Sew piece **a** between the bun units as shown.

17 To make the face, take an **f** piece of Fabric 2 and using an erasable marker, mark the ¼in (6mm) seam allowance all round. Mark four dots on the seam line in the positions indicated in **Fig L 1**. Take a **g** piece of Fabric 1 and mark the ¼in (6mm) seam allowance all round. Mark two dots on the marked line, as shown, and also a diagonal line from corner to corner of the inner shape. Place the fabric pieces right sides together as in **Fig L 2**, carefully angling the small rectangle so the dots on the diagonal line are matched with the dots on the fabric below. Pin in place and then sew along the marked diagonal line (you can sew past the ends of the line if you want). Press the triangle into place (**Fig L 3**). Repeat this process with a second **g** piece, sewing it to the opposite side of piece **f**, as in **Fig L 4**. Trim excess fabric.

18 To add the hair take an **i** piece of Fabric 3 and create a corner triangle on the face unit (**Fig L 5**), using the same method as before. Trim excess fabric. Repeat with an **h** piece on the opposite side of the face unit (**Fig L 6**). Shape the hair by using two **j** pieces of Fabric 1 to create corner triangles (**Fig L 7** and **L 8**).

19 Make the neck area using a **k** piece of Fabric 2 and two **l** squares of Fabric 1. Create corner triangles using the same method as before. Press, trim excess fabric and then sew this unit to the bottom of the face unit (**Fig L 9**). Assemble the head section following **Fig M**.

20 Making the shoulder and wing unit: Start by making the HSTs, taking a 3⅜in (8.6cm) **b** square of Fabric 1 and one of Fabric 27 (for Angel block 1). Make the units as described in Step 7. This time, each HST unit should be 3in (7.6cm) square (unfinished).

21 Make a shoulder section by using one **c** piece of Fabric 27 and one **d** piece of Fabric 2. Create the triangle shape in the same way that you did for the face, this time following **Fig N**. Make a second shoulder section facing the opposite way.

Fig K Making the hair buns

Fig M Assembling the head section

Fig L Making the face and neck

1¾in (4.4cm) 1¾in (4.4cm) 1in (2.5cm) 1in (2.5cm)

22 Take piece **f** of Fabric 23 and two of piece **g** of Fabric 27 and create corner triangles on the top of the long rectangle. Now assemble the shoulder and wing section following **Fig O**.

23 Making the dress unit: Start with the centre section, sewing together pieces **a**, **b**, **c** and **c** (see **Fig P**). Now take square **f** and create a triangle on the bottom right corner of piece **e**, using the corner triangle method, as before. Sew piece **d** to the left-hand side of the **e/f** unit. Repeat this to create another **d/e/f** unit but this time facing the opposite way.

24 For the curved sides of the skirt on the left-hand side, use the full-size patterns to mark and then cut shapes **g**, **h**, **i** and **j** accurately from the relevant fabrics. Seam allowances are included on the patterns. For the curved sides of the skirt on the right-hand side reverse (flip) the patterns to cut these **g**, **h**, **i** and **j** shapes.

25 Sew pieces **g**, **h** and **i** together, aligning straight edges, and press (Fig P). Sew piece **j** to this **g/h/i** unit, pinning the curves together to achieve a smooth, curved sewing line. Sew the **d/e/f** unit to the top of the curved section. Repeat this process to sew the opposite **g/h/i/j** unit. Now sew the three columns of the dress together.

26 Making the legs unit: Take the two **c** squares of Fabric 1 and create corner triangles on the bottom of the two **b** pieces. Now sew the pieces for the leg unit together in this order – **a**, **b/c**, **d**, **b/c**, **a**.

27 To assemble the Angel block, sew all of the units for the block together. The block should be 16½in x 35in (42cm x 89cm) at this stage. Repeat this whole process to make an Angel 2 block and then an Angel 3 block, following the fabric positions in **Fig I**.

MAKING THE SASHING

28 There are five sashing layouts – sashing 1 and sashing 5 are unpieced strips of Fabric 1, while sashing 2, sashing 3 and sashing 4 are pieced with plum units and pinwheel units. **Fig Q** shows these units and the fabrics needed. Make the plum units as you did before – see **Fig D** for the sizes of fabric to cut and **Fig F** for assembling a unit.

Fig N Making the shoulder

1¾in
(4.4cm)

Fig O Assembling the shoulder and wing section

Fig P Sewing the skirt and assembling the dress

29 To make a pinwheel unit, cut a 2½in (6.4cm) square of Fabric 1 and Fabric 25 and use these to make HSTs, as before. Check each HST is 2⅛in (5.4cm) square. Repeat this to make two HSTs from Fabric 1 and Fabric 23. Arrange the four HSTs as in **Fig Q**, sewing them together in pairs and then sewing the pairs together. The unit should be 3¾in (9.5cm) at this stage. Make another pinwheel unit like this. Make two more pinwheel units but this time using Fabric 1, Fabric 25 and Fabric 21.

30 To assemble the sashing units, start by cutting the pieces of Fabric 1 given in **Fig R**. Lay out the strips and the plum and pinwheel units in the positions shown and then sew each sashing unit together.

MAKING THE FLAG BORDERS

31 There are two of these borders (H1 and H2 on **Fig B**). They are identical except that the colours of the flying geese units are reversed in lower border H2. For each border cut the following pieces.
- Fabric 25 – two strips 28in x 1¼in (71.1cm x 3.2cm) and sew together. (If you prefer, you could join shorter strips, as long as the total length is 55½in/141cm when joined.)
- Fabric 1 – four strips 28in x 2in (71.1cm x 5.1cm). Sew two strips together into one strip. Repeat with the other two strips.
- Fabric 1 – two pieces 3½in x 6¾in (9cm x 17.1cm).
- Fabric 1 – twenty-two squares 3in (7.6cm) for flying geese.
- Two rectangles 3in x 5½in (7.6cm x 14cm) from each of Fabrics 11, 16, 12, 7 and 19.
- One rectangle 3in x 5½in (7.6cm x 14cm) of Fabric 10.

32 To make one flying geese unit you will need two 3in (7.6cm) squares of Fabric 1 and a 5½in x 3in (14cm x 7.6cm) rectangle of a print fabric. Make a flying geese unit following the instructions in Basic Techniques: Flying Geese Unit. Check the sewn unit is 5½in x 3in (14cm x 7.6cm). Make eleven flying geese like this for each border.

33 Once the flying geese are made, sew the flag border together as shown in **Fig S**. Repeat this for the other flag border but arrange the flying geese so the fabrics are mirrored the opposite way.

ASSEMBLING THE QUILT

34 Before sewing the sections of the quilt together, make six appliqué cheeks for the angels. Using the circle pattern provided, cutting six 1½in (3.8cm) circles from Fabric 4. Follow the instructions in Basic Techniques: Appliqué: Gathering Over Card Method. Sew the cheeks into place on the angels, using matching thread and tiny stitches.

35 Lay out all the sections of the quilt, following **Fig B** carefully. For the top border cut two Fabric 1 strips each 31in x 2in (78.7cm x 5.1cm) and sew together. Sew the top section of the quilt together and press. Add one of the flag borders to the bottom. Repeat with the bottom sections of the quilt. Sew the two large sections together and add the Fabric 1 top border strip to the top to finish.

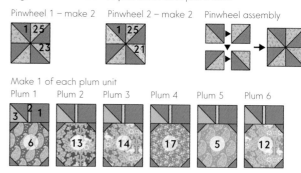

Fig Q Fabrics used for pinwheel and plum units

Pinwheel 1 – make 2   Pinwheel 2 – make 2   Pinwheel assembly

Make 1 of each plum unit
Plum 1   Plum 2   Plum 3   Plum 4   Plum 5   Plum 6

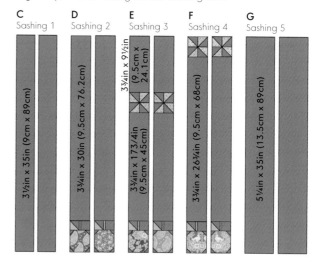

Fig R Layout and cutting for the sashing units

C Sashing 1   D Sashing 2   E Sashing 3   F Sashing 4   G Sashing 5

3½in x 35in (9cm x 89cm)

3¾in x 30in (9.5cm x 76.2cm)

3¾in x 9½in (9.5cm x 24.1cm)

3¾in x 17¾in (9.5cm x 45cm)

3¾in x 26¾in (9.5cm x 68cm)

5¼in x 35in (13.5cm x 89cm)

Fig S Assembling a flag border
Numbers indicate fabrics used.
Flag border H2 is identical to H1 but the flying geese fabrics are arranged the opposite way

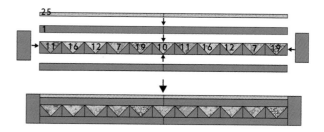

QUILTING AND FINISHING

36 Make a quilt sandwich of the backing fabric, wadding (batting) and quilt. Quilt as desired. Square up the quilt, trimming excess wadding and backing.

37 Use the prepared double-fold binding strip to bind your quilt (see Basic Techniques: Binding). Add a label and your quilt is finished.

COSY STRIPE QUILT

This quilt is very easy to make as it is just blocks of rectangles separated by strips of vertical sashing. The print rectangles can be cut from a fat eighth, which is assumed to be at least 10½in x 18in (26.7cm x 45.7cm). You can also make a pillow for this quilt – see end of chapter.

MATERIALS

- Fabric 1: fat eighth – Teardrop peach
- Fabric 2: fat eighth – Windflower red
- Fabric 3: fat eighth – Flower Confetti sand
- Fabric 4: fat eighth – Autumn Bouquet peach
- Fabric 5: fat eighth – Duck Nest peach
- Fabric 6: fat eighth – Windflower lavender
- Fabric 7: fat eighth – Flower Confetti plum
- Fabric 8: fat eighth – Teardrop plum
- Fabric 9: fat eighth – Duck Nest plum
- Fabric 10: fat eighth – Autumn Bouquet lavender
- Fabric 11: fat eighth – Windflower blueberry
- Fabric 12: fat eighth – Flower Confetti blue
- Fabric 13: fat eighth – Duck Nest blueberry
- Fabric 14: fat eighth – Autumn Bouquet teal
- Fabric 15: fat eighth – Teardrop blueberry
- Fabric 16: fat eighth – Autumn Bouquet blue
- Fabric 17: fat eighth – Duck Nest nutmeg
- Fabric 18: fat eighth – Teardrop nutmeg
- Fabric 19: fat eighth – Windflower nutmeg
- Fabric 20: fat eighth – Flower Confetti nutmeg
- Fabric 21: ⅜yd (40cm) – Cinnamon Roll Plaid plum
- Fabric 22: ½yd (50cm) – Cantucci Stripe plum
- Fabric 23: ½yd (50cm) – Brownie Stripe plum
- Backing fabric 3⅜yd (3m)
- Wadding (batting) 59in x 79in (150cm x 200.6cm)
- Binding fabric ½yd (50cm) – Berry Jam teal

Finished Size 50in x 70in (127cm x 178cm)

Fig A Fabric swatches – if you can't source a fabric, replace with one in a similar colour

Fabric 1
Teardrop peach

Fabric 9
Duck Nest plum

Fabric 17
Duck Nest nutmeg

Fabric 2
Windflower red

Fabric 10
Autumn Bouquet lavender

Fabric 18
Teardrop nutmeg

Fabric 3
Flower Confetti sand

Fabric 11
Windflower blueberry

Fabric 19
Windflower nutmeg

Fabric 4
Autumn Bouquet peach

Fabric 12
Flower Confetti blue

Fabric 20
Flower Confetti nutmeg

Fabric 5
Duck Nest peach

Fabric 13
Duck Nest blueberry

Fabric 21
Cinnamon Roll Plaid plum

Fabric 6
Windflower lavender

Fabric 14
Autumn Bouquet teal

Fabric 22
Cantucci Stripe plum

Fabric 7
Flower Confetti plum

Fabric 15
Teardrop blueberry

Fabric 23
Brownie Stripe plum

Fabric 8
Teardrop plum

Fabric 16
Autumn Bouquet blue

PREPARATION AND CUTTING OUT

1 Before you start, refer to Basic Techniques: Making Quilts and Pillows. The quilt is made up of repeating rectangular blocks joined into columns. Each block is made up of five different print fabrics and there are four different blocks. The fabrics used for the quilt are shown in **Fig A** and the quilt layout in **Fig B**.

2 To cut the rectangles for the blocks, follow **Fig C**. Each individual rectangle needs to be cut 4½in x 2½in (11.4cm x 6.4cm). Cut fourteen rectangles from each of Fabrics 1 to 20. Arrange the rectangles in groups as shown in the diagram.

Fig B Quilt layout

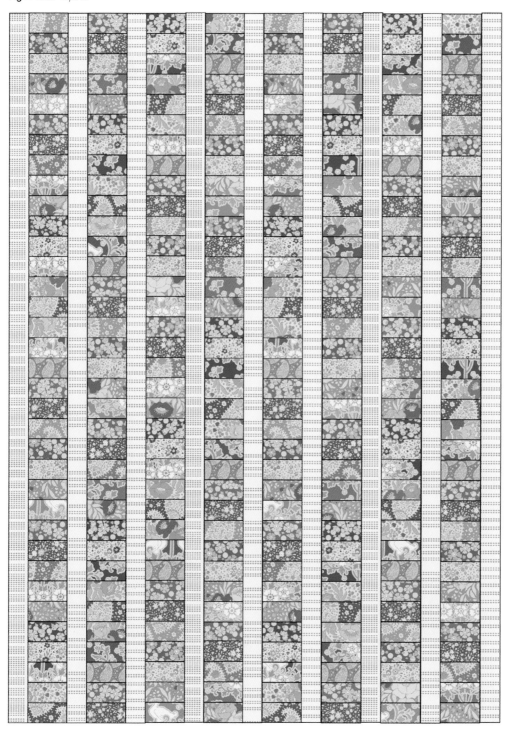

3 The vertical sashing strips are 2½in (6.4cm) wide and use Fabrics 21, 22 and 23 in a repeating pattern – see **Fig D**. From Fabric 21 cut six strips 2½in (6.4cm) x width of fabric. Join these together end to end to make a strip at least 212in (538.5cm) long. Now sub-cut this into three strips each 2½in x 70½in (6.4cm x 179cm). Repeat this cutting and sewing with strips of Fabric 22 and Fabric 23.

4 Cut the backing fabric in half across the width. Sew together along the long side and trim to a piece about 59in x 79in (150cm x 200.6cm).

5 From the binding fabric cut seven strips 2½in (6.4cm) x width of fabric. Sew together end to end and press seams open. Press in half along the length, wrong sides together.

SEWING THE BLOCKS

6 Take the five rectangles for Block 1 (Fabrics 1, 2, 3, 4 and 5) and sew them together into a column (**Fig E**). Press the seams in one direction. Repeat with the pieces for Block 2, Block 3 and Block 4. Repeat until you have fourteen of each block.

Fig C Cutting the block fabrics
Cut each rectangle 4½in x 2½in (11.4cm x 6.4cm)
Bold numbers indicate fabrics
Cut 14 from each fabric

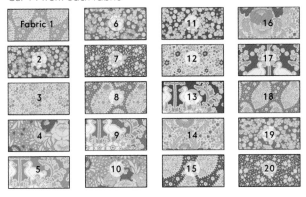

Fig D Cutting the sashing
Cut each strip 2½in x 70½in (6.4cm x 179cm),
joining as needed
Bold numbers indicate fabrics
Make 3 from each fabric

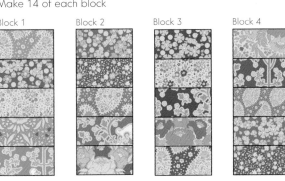

Fig E Making the blocks
Make 14 of each block

Block 1   Block 2   Block 3   Block 4

Fig F Sewing a column for the quilt

Fig G Adding the sashing

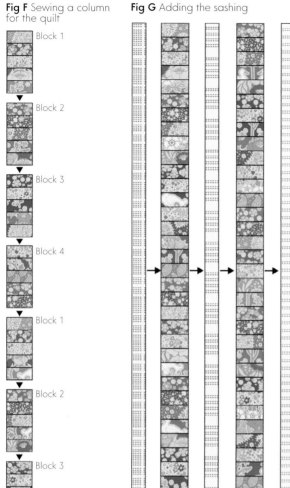

Block 1

Block 2

Block 3

Block 4

Block 1

Block 2

Block 3

ASSEMBLING THE QUILT

7 Follow **Fig F** to arrange seven blocks as shown (Block 1, 2, 3, 4, 1, 2, 3). Sew them together and press seams in one direction. Repeat this to sew the other seven columns of the quilt, following the quilt layout in **Fig B** for the order of the blocks.

8 Lay out the sewn columns with the sashing strips between them and at each end. Note that the order of the sashing repeats from the left-hand side of the quilt. Begin sewing the sashing strips to the columns of blocks, as in **Fig G**, pressing the seams in one direction.

QUILTING AND FINISHING

9 Make a quilt sandwich of the backing fabric, wadding (batting) and quilt. Quilt as desired. Square up the quilt, trimming excess wadding and backing.

10 Use the prepared double-fold binding strip to bind your quilt (see Basic Techniques: Binding). Add a label and your quilt is finished.

COSY STRIPE PILLOW

You can use the same sizes of rectangle and fabrics to make a matching pillow for the quilt. Sew fifteen rectangles together into a column and make five columns like this. Cut two sashing strips 2½in x 30½in (6.4cm x 77.5cm) from each of three fabrics. Sew these between the rectangle columns and at each end, as shown in **Fig A** here, and then press. Add wadding (batting) and then quilt the patchwork. Make up as a bound pillow as described in Basic Techniques: Bound-Edge Pillow Cover. Insert a pad to finish.

Fig A Sewing the pillow together

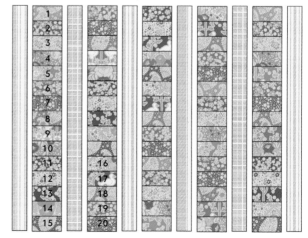

PLUM GARDEN VILLAGE QUILT

This charming quilt is easier to make than it seems, creating a bright and fresh quilt that will look good all year long. Decorative extras in the form of patterned buttons and sweet little appliquéd bees add a special touch. A lovely pillow can be made for the quilt – see next chapter.

MATERIALS

- Fabric 1: fat eighth – Duck Nest plum
- Fabric 2: fat eighth – Berry Jam peach
- Fabric 3: fat eighth – Windflower red
- Fabric 4: fat eighth – Brownie Stripe plum
- Fabric 5: fat eighth – Spongecake Stripe teal
- Fabric 6: fat eighth – Teardrop plum
- Fabric 7: fat eighth – Flower Confetti sand
- Fabric 8: fat eighth – Windflower lavender
- Fabric 9: fat eighth – Autumn Bouquet peach
- Fabric 10: fat eighth – Flower Confetti plum
- Fabric 11: fat eighth – Scone Stripe teal
- Fabric 12: fat eighth – Plum Dot dove white
- Fabric 13: fat eighth – Duck Nest peach
- Fabric 14: fat eighth – Berry Jam plum
- Fabric 15: fat eighth – Autumn Bouquet lavender
- Fabric 16: fat eighth – Teardrop peach
- Fabric 17: fat eighth – Duck Nest blueberry
- Fabric 18: ⅞yd (60cm) – Biscotti Plaid teal
- Fabric 19: fat eighth – Flower Confetti nutmeg
- Fabric 20: fat eighth – Berry Jam wicker
- Fabric 21: fat eighth – Windflower blueberry
- Fabric 22: fat eighth – Teardrop nutmeg
- Fabric 23: fat eighth – Autumn Bouquet blue
- Fabric 24: fat eighth – Duck Nest nutmeg
- Fabric 25: fat eighth – Flower Confetti blue
- Fabric 26: fat eighth – Teardrop blueberry
- Fabric 27: fat eighth – Berry Jam blue
- Fabric 28: fat eighth – Windflower nutmeg
- Fabric 29: fat eighth – Autumn Bouquet teal
- Fabric 30: fat eighth – Plum Dot nutmeg
- Fabric 31: ¼yd (25cm) or fat quarter – Berry Jam teal
- Fabric 32: 3in (7.6cm) square – Macaron Plaid blue
- Fabric 33: 1⅜yd (1.25m) – Solid dove white
- Backing fabric 3⅜yd (3m)
- Wadding (batting) 59in x 71in (150cm x 180cm)
- Binding fabric ½yd (50cm) – Berry Jam peach
- Embroidery cotton (floss) for bee trails (optional)
- Thick paper and fabric glue for bee paper piece appliqué
- Tilda buttons (see Step 19)

Fig A Fabric swatches – if you can't source a fabric, replace with one in a similar colour

Fabric 1
Duck Nest plum

Fabric 12
Plum Dot dove white

Fabric 23
Autumn Bouquet blue

Fabric 2
Berry Jam peach

Fabric 13
Duck Nest peach

Fabric 24
Duck Nest nutmeg

Fabric 3
Windflower red

Fabric 14
Berry Jam plum

Fabric 25
Flower Confetti blue

Fabric 4
Brownie Stripe plum

Fabric 15
Autumn Bouquet lavender

Fabric 26
Teardrop blueberry

Fabric 5
Spongecake Stripe teal

Fabric 16
Teardrop peach

Fabric 27
Berry Jam blue

Fabric 6
Teardrop plum

Fabric 17
Duck Nest blueberry

Fabric 28
Windflower nutmeg

Fabric 7
Flower Confetti sand

Fabric 18
Biscotti Plaid teal

Fabric 29
Autumn Bouquet teal

Fabric 8
Windflower lavender

Fabric 19
Flower Confetti nutmeg

Fabric 30
Plum Dot nutmeg

Fabric 9
Autumn Bouquet peach

Fabric 20
Berry Jam wicker

Fabric 31
Berry Jam teal

Fabric 10
Flower Confetti plum

Fabric 21
Windflower blueberry

Fabric 32
Macaron Plaid blue

Fabric 11
Scone Stripe teal

Fabric 22
Teardrop nutmeg

Fabric 33
Solid dove white

Finished Size 50in x 62½in (127cm x 159cm)

Fabric Note Only fat eighths, (10½in x 18in (26.7cm x 45.7cm), can be used where stated in the Materials list – a long ⅛yd *cannot* be used.

PREPARATION AND CUTTING OUT

1 Before you start, refer to Basic Techniques: Making Quilts and Pillows. This quilt is made up of two main blocks sewn together in rows – a Tree block and a House block, with the houses of two types. The Tree blocks are separated by vertical sashing in two different widths. The house rows are separated by narrow horizontal sashing. There is also a narrow sashing border and a wider outer border. The fabrics used are shown in **Fig A** and the quilt layout in **Fig B**.

2 **Fig C** shows the layout and cutting for the house blocks, and **Fig D** for the Tree block, so use these measurements to cut out the fabrics for a block. Measurements include ¼in (6mm) seam allowances. The House blocks are made in rows of seven houses. These rows and their colourways are shown in **Fig E**. Make three each of House Rows 1 and 2 and two each of House Rows 3 and 4.

There are only two colourways for the Tree blocks – see **Fig F**.

Fig B Quilt layout

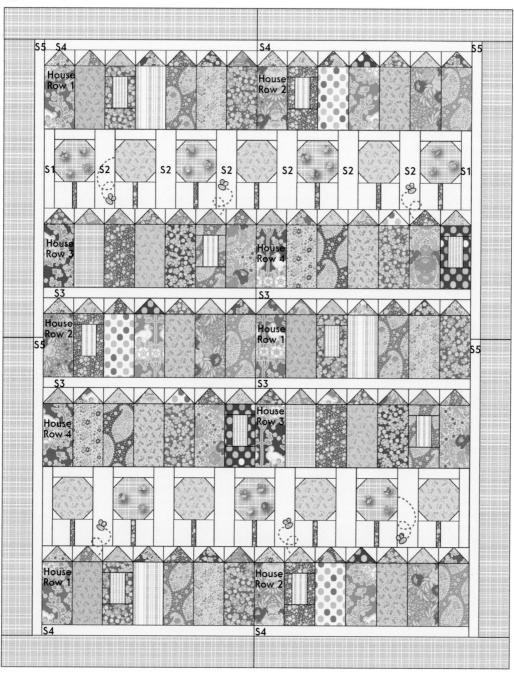

3 All of the sashing is cut from Fabric 33. **Fig B** identifies the pieces. For the tree row sashing cut the following pieces.

- S1 – four 1½in x 8in (3.8cm x 20.3cm).
- S2 – twelve 2½in x 8in (6.4cm x 20.3cm).

For the horizontal sashing between the house rows cut four strips of S3, each 21½in x 1½in (54.6cm x 3.8cm). Join the strips together in pairs. (Note: When selvedges are removed from the solid fabric you may have a width of 42½in (108cm), which means that you could cut just two width-of-fabric strips, with no joins.)

For the sashing border cut the following strips.

- S4 – four 21½in x 1½in (54.6cm x 3.8cm) for the top and bottom of the quilt. Join the strips together in pairs (see note above about using width-of-fabric strips).
- S5 – four 1½in x 28¾in (3.8cm x 73cm) for the sides of the quilt. Join the strips together in pairs.

4 The outer border is cut from Fabric 18. Cut the following strips.

- Four strips 3½in x 28¾in (9cm x 73cm) for the sides of the quilt. Join the strips together in pairs.
- Four strips 25½in x 3½in (64.8cm x 9cm) for the top and bottom of the quilt. Join the strips together in pairs.

5 Cut the backing fabric in half across the width. Sew the pieces together along the long side. Press the seam open and trim to a piece about 59in x 71in (150cm x 180cm).

6 From the binding fabric cut six strips 2½in (6.4cm) x width of fabric. Sew together end to end and press the seams open. Press in half along the length, wrong sides together.

MAKING THE HOUSE BLOCKS

7 There are two types of house – one plain and one with a window. Both types have a roof made from a flying geese unit. The unit for the first house in House Row 1 will be described here. Take one 3½in x 2in (9cm x 5.1cm) rectangle (**a**) of Fabric 23 and two 2in (5.1cm) squares (**b**) of Fabric 33 and follow the instructions in Basic Techniques: Flying Geese Unit. Make all roofs this way, changing fabrics as needed.

8 Assemble a plain house by sewing the flying geese unit on top of the **c** rectangle. The block should be 3½in x 8in (9cm x 20.3cm) at this stage. Make sixty plain house blocks in total, changing fabrics as in **Fig E**.

Fig C Layout and cutting for the House blocks

House　　**House with window**

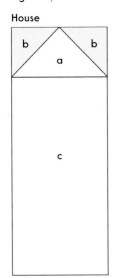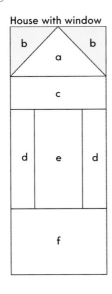

Fig D Layout and cutting for the Tree block

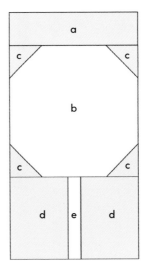

House
a 3½in x 2in (9cm x 5.1cm).
b 2in (5.1cm) square.
c 3½in x 6½in (9cm x 16.5cm).

House with window
a 3½in x 2in (9cm x 5.1cm).
b 2in (5.1cm) square.
c 3½in x 1½in (9cm x 3.8cm).
d 1¼in x 3½in (3.2cm x 9cm).
e 2in x 3½in (5.1cm x 9cm).
f 3½in x 2½in (9cm x 6.4cm).

Tree
a 4½in x 1½in (11.4cm x 3.8cm).
b 4½in (11.4cm) square.
c 1½in (3.8cm) square.
d 2⅜in x 3in (6cm x 7.6cm).
e ¾in x 3in (2cm x 7.6cm).

Fig E Fabrics used for the House blocks
Bold numbers indicate fabrics used (see **Fig A**)

House Row 1 – make 3

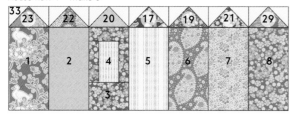

House Row 2 – make 3

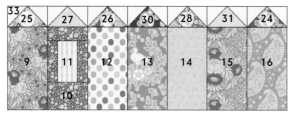

House Row 3 – make 2

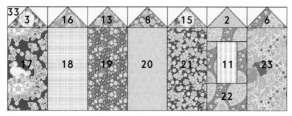

House Row 4 – make 2

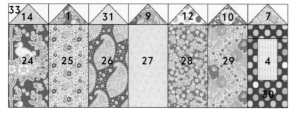

9 The house with a window needs more pieces, so follow **Fig G** for the sequence of sewing. Start by sewing a piece **d** to both sides of piece **e**. Press the seams. Add piece **c** to the top and piece **f** to the bottom and press. Make a roof unit, sew it to the top of the block and press. The block should be 3½in x 8in (9cm x 20.3cm) at this stage. Make ten blocks like this in total, changing fabrics as in **Fig E**.

10 Sew seven house blocks in a row. Press the seams in one direction. Assemble the rest of the house rows, following **Fig E** for the positions of the blocks and the number of rows to make.

MAKING A TREE BLOCK

11 All of the Tree blocks are made the same way. The only difference is the centre fabric, which is either Fabric 18 or Fabric 31. Pencil mark the diagonal line on the wrong side of four 1½in (3.8cm) **c** squares of solid Fabric 33. Place these squares right sides together with a 4½in (11.4cm) **b** square of Fabric 18, as in **Fig H 1**. Pin if needed and then sew along the marked lines as shown. Trim off excess fabric ¼in (6mm) outside the sewn line and press the little triangles outwards.

Sew the tree trunk unit by adding one **d** rectangle to each side of a narrow **e** rectangle and press the seams (**Fig H 2**).

Sew rectangle **a** to the top of the tree unit, add the trunk unit to the bottom (**Fig H 3**) and then press seams. The block should be 4½in x 8in (11.4cm x 20.3cm) at this stage.

12 Using the same process, make seven of Tree block 1 and seven of Tree block 2.

For the upper tree row in the quilt take four of Tree 1 and three of Tree 2 and lay them out alternately with S2 sashing pieces between them and S1 sashing pieces at the ends of the row. Sew the pieces together and press the seams in one direction. Make another row like this but this time begin with Tree 2.

Fig F Fabrics used for the Tree blocks
Bold numbers indicate fabrics used

Tree 1 – make 7   Tree 2 – make 7

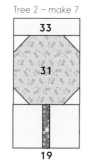

Fig G Making a house with window

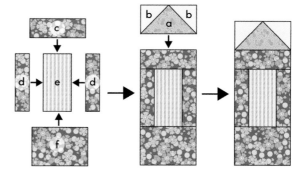

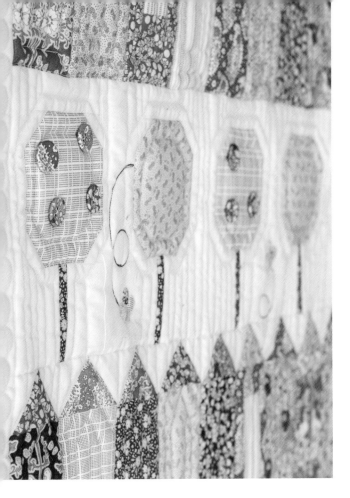

ASSEMBLING THE QUILT

13 The quilt is assembled in rows. Start by sewing the house block rows together, as follows.
- House Row 1 + House Row 2.
- House Row 3 + House Row 4.
- House Row 2 + House Row 1.
- House Row 4 + House Row 3.
- House Row 1 + House Row 2.

14 Follow **Fig I** to begin sewing the rows of the quilt together. Now follow the main quilt layout in **Fig B** to add the rest of the rows.

15 Add the inner sashing border following **Fig J**, sewing the S4 strips to the top and bottom of the quilt. Press seams outwards. Add the S5 strips to the sides of the quilt and press outwards.

16 Now add the outer border following **Fig K**, sewing the strips to the sides of the quilt first, and then the top and bottom of the quilt. Press seams outwards.

Fig J Adding the inner sashing border

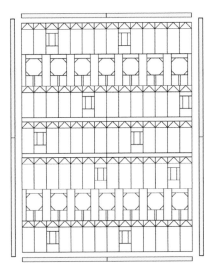

Fig H Making a Tree block

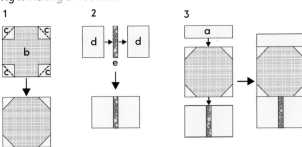

Fig K Adding the outer border

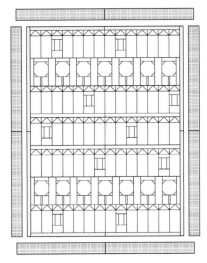

Fig I Beginning to assemble the quilt centre

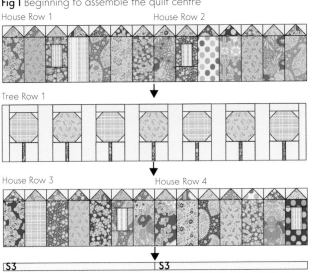

ADDING THE BEE APPLIQUÉS

17 To make the bees a paper pieced method was used, folding the edge of the fabric over a paper pattern (see **Fig L**). For each bee you will need one body (Fabric 20) and two wings (Fabric 25 and 32). Follow the instructions in Basic Techniques: Applique: Paper Piece Method. Make the wings using the same technique. Make six bees like this in total.

18 Sew the bees into place on the tree rows of the quilt, using matching thread and tiny stitches, arranging the bees so some face left and some face right and overlapping the pieces as in **Fig M**. The bee 'flight paths' or trails can either be sewn with machine quilting or with hand embroidery. **Fig N** shows the curling shapes of these stitches, but you can mark your own if you prefer. If using hand embroidery, use running stitch and two or three strands of embroidery thread in a colour to suit the quilt, perhaps medium brown or grey.

19 Buttons have been added to some of the trees but it is best to wait until all quilting is finished before adding these. We used two packs each of Tilda ¾in (20mm) buttons (400025) and ⅝in (17mm) buttons (400024). Some trees have three buttons and some four, with the sizes mixed. Twenty-four buttons were used but you could use more. **Fig B** shows the positions but you could choose your own places. Sew the buttons in place with a pale thread and finish off neatly and securely at the back of the quilt.

QUILTING AND FINISHING

20 Make a quilt sandwich of the backing fabric, wadding (batting) and quilt. Quilt as desired. Square up the quilt, trimming excess wadding and backing.

21 Use the prepared double-fold binding strip to bind your quilt (see Basic Techniques: Binding). Add a label and your quilt is finished.

Fig L Making the bee appliqué

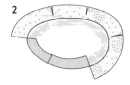

Fig M Arranging the bees

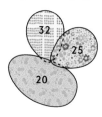

Bee facing left   Bee facing right

Fig N Sewing the bee trails

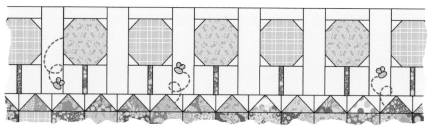

Top tree row – direction of bee trails   Bottom tree row – direction of bee trails

PLUM VILLAGE PILLOW

Why not make this pretty pillow to accompany the Plum Garden Village Quilt? It features the same blocks as the quilt but in different colours and you only need to make one row of houses and one row of trees. It uses some of the same fabrics as the quilt, so refer to the fabric swatches in **Fig A** of the quilt instructions.

MATERIALS

- Fabric 1: 3½in x 6½in (9cm x 16.5cm) – Duck Nest plum
- Fabric 3: 8in (20.3cm) square – Windflower red
- Fabric 4: 3½in x 2in (9cm x 5.1cm) – Brownie Stripe plum
- Fabric 6: 3½in x 6½in (9cm x 16.5cm) – Teardrop plum
- Fabric 8: 3½in x 6½in (9cm x 16.5cm) – Windflower lavender
- Fabric 11: 3½in x 2in (9cm x 5.1cm) – Scone Stripe teal
- Fabric 12: 3½in x 6½in (9cm x 16.5cm) – Plum Dot dove white
- Fabric 13: 8in (20.3cm) square – Duck Nest peach
- Fabric 16: two 4½in (11.4cm) squares – Teardrop peach
- Fabric 17: 3½in x 2in (9cm x 5.1cm) – Duck Nest blueberry
- Fabric 18: ⅜yd (40cm) – Biscotti Plaid teal
- Fabric 19: 5in (12.7cm) square – Flower Confetti nutmeg
- Fabric 20: 10in (25.4cm) square – Berry Jam wicker
- Fabric 21: 3½in x 2in (9cm x 5.1cm) – Windflower blueberry
- Fabric 22: 3½in x 2in (9cm x 5.1cm) – Teardrop nutmeg
- Fabric 23: 3½in x 2in (9cm x 5.1cm) – Autumn Bouquet blue
- Fabric 25: 8in (20.3cm) square – Flower Confetti blue
- Fabric 29: 3½in x 2in (9cm x 5.1cm) – Autumn Bouquet teal
- Fabric 31: 3½in x 6½in (9cm x 16.5cm) – Berry Jam teal
- Wadding (batting) 27½in x 17½in (70cm x 44.5cm)
- Lining fabric 27½in x 17½in (70cm x 44.5cm) (optional)
- Fabric for back of pillow, two pieces 16½in (42cm) square
- Binding fabric ¼yd (25cm) – Berry Jam peach
- One pack of nine Tilda ⅝in (17mm) buttons (400024)
- Pad to fit pillow cover

Finished Size 26in x 16in (66cm x 40.6cm)

PREPARATION AND CUTTING OUT

1 The pillow uses the same blocks as the quilt, made the same way. Use **Fig C** of the quilt to cut the pieces for the houses and **Fig D** to cut the pieces for a tree. The fabrics to use are different to the quilt and are shown in **Fig A** here. Use Fabric 18 for the sashing, cutting the following pieces.
- Two 1½in x 8in (3.8cm x 20.3cm).
- Five 2½in x 8in (6.4cm x 20.3cm).
- One 26½in x 1½in (67.3cm x 3.8cm).

2 From the binding fabric cut three strips 2½in (6.4cm) x width of fabric. Sew together, press seams open and prepare as a double-fold binding.

MAKING THE HOUSES

3 To make the house blocks, follow the quilt instructions (Steps 7 to 9) for six plain houses and two houses with a window. Sew them together in a row with a 1½in x 8in (3.8cm x 20.3cm) piece of sashing at each end and press seams.

MAKING THE TREES

4 To make the four tree blocks, follow the quilt instructions (Step 11). Sew them together in a row with 2½in x 8in (6.4cm x 20.3cm) pieces of sashing between each block and at each end and press seams.

ASSEMBLING, QUILTING AND MAKING UP

5 Lay out the house row and the tree row, with the long strip of sashing above the houses, as in **Fig A** here. Sew the rows together and press seams. The patchwork should be 26½in x 16½in (67.3cm x 42cm).

6 Make a quilt sandwich and quilt as desired. Trim excess fabric to match the patchwork size. Sew the buttons in position on two of the tree blocks. Make up as a bound pillow as described in Basic Techniques: Bound-Edge Pillow Cover.

Fig A Assembling the pillow

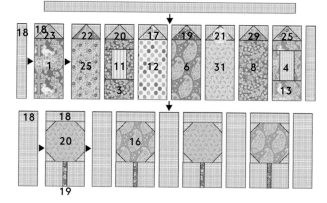

PLUM QUILT

A single block in four different colourways and some paper piece appliqué is all that it takes to make this pretty quilt in soft peach, plum, blue and nutmeg colours. The curves needed to create the plums are quite easy to piece with the patterns supplied.

MATERIALS

- Fabric 1: ¼yd (25cm) – Teardrop peach
- Fabric 2: ¼yd (25cm) – Autumn Bouquet peach
- Fabric 3: ¼yd (25cm) – Duck Nest peach
- Fabric 4: ¼yd (25cm) – Flower Confetti sand
- Fabric 5: ¼yd (25cm) – Duck Nest nutmeg
- Fabric 6: ¼yd (25cm) – Windflower nutmeg
- Fabric 7: ¼yd (25cm) – Teardrop nutmeg
- Fabric 8: ¼yd (25cm) – Autumn Bouquet blue
- Fabric 9: ¼yd (25cm) – Autumn Bouquet teal
- Fabric 10: ¼yd (25cm) – Teardrop blueberry
- Fabric 11: ¼yd (25cm) – Duck Nest blueberry
- Fabric 12: ¼yd (25cm) – Flower Confetti blue
- Fabric 13: ¼yd (25cm) – Windflower lavender
- Fabric 14: ¼yd (25cm) – Duck Nest plum
- Fabric 15: ¼yd (25cm) – Autumn Bouquet lavender
- Fabric 16: ¼yd (25cm) – Teardrop plum
- Fabric 17: 5in (12.7cm) square – Berry Jam plum
- Fabric 18: 12in (30.5cm) square – Windflower blueberry
- Fabric 19: 5in (12.7cm) square – Berry Jam peach
- Fabric 20: 12in (30.5cm) square – Flower Confetti plum
- Fabric 21: 5in (12.7cm) square – Berry Jam wicker
- Fabric 22: 12in (30.5cm) square – Windflower red
- Fabric 23: 5in (12.7cm) square – Berry Jam blue
- Fabric 24: 12in (30.5cm) square – Flower Confetti nutmeg
- Fabric 25: 1yd (1m) – Spongecake Stripe teal
- Fabric 26: 1yd (1m) – Scone Stripe teal
- Backing fabric 3½yd (3.25m)
- Wadding (batting) 59in x 76in (150cm x 193cm)
- Binding fabric ½yd (50cm) – Plum Dot dove white
- Thick paper to make templates
- Fabric glue for paper piece appliqué

Finished Size 50in x 67in (127cm x 170.2cm)

Fig A Fabric swatches – if you can't source a fabric, replace with one in a similar colour

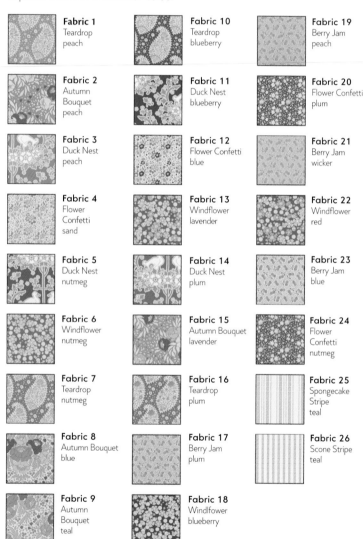

Fabric 1 Teardrop peach
Fabric 2 Autumn Bouquet peach
Fabric 3 Duck Nest peach
Fabric 4 Flower Confetti sand
Fabric 5 Duck Nest nutmeg
Fabric 6 Windflower nutmeg
Fabric 7 Teardrop nutmeg
Fabric 8 Autumn Bouquet blue
Fabric 9 Autumn Bouquet teal
Fabric 10 Teardrop blueberry
Fabric 11 Duck Nest blueberry
Fabric 12 Flower Confetti blue
Fabric 13 Windflower lavender
Fabric 14 Duck Nest plum
Fabric 15 Autumn Bouquet lavender
Fabric 16 Teardrop plum
Fabric 17 Berry Jam plum
Fabric 18 Windlfower blueberry
Fabric 19 Berry Jam peach
Fabric 20 Flower Confetti plum
Fabric 21 Berry Jam wicker
Fabric 22 Windflower red
Fabric 23 Berry Jam blue
Fabric 24 Flower Confetti nutmeg
Fabric 25 Spongecake Stripe teal
Fabric 26 Scone Stripe teal

Fabric Note Where a long ¼yd is given in the Materials list you could use a fat quarter instead, which is assumed to be approximately 21in x 18in (53.3cm x 45.7cm).

PREPARATION AND CUTTING OUT

1 Before you start, refer to Basic Techniques: Making Quilts and Pillows. There are 25 blocks in the quilt, all made the same way but in four different colourways. The top row of the quilt is made up of simple rectangular units. The fabrics used for the quilt are shown in **Fig A** and the quilt layout in **Fig B**.

2 Each block has four units, with each unit made up of two curved pieces, created from patterns A and B. Copy the patterns onto thick paper (seam allowances are included). In the diagram given with the patterns, you will see that some shapes in a block need to be cut with the patterns rotated 180 degrees, some with the patterns reversed

Fig B Quilt layout

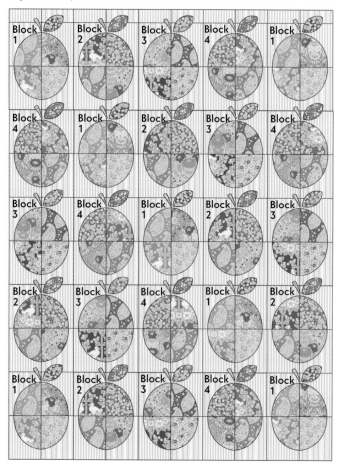

Fig C Pattern pieces needed
Bold numbers indicate fabrics
Rotate and/or reverse the paper patterns
as needed

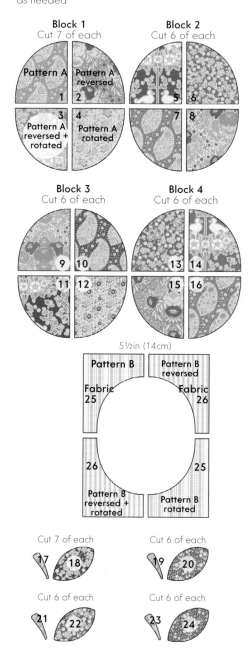

(flipped) and some with the patterns reversed and rotated. Print out or copy the patterns, making sure they are full size. Pattern A should be 4¾in x 5½in (12cm x 14cm) including seam allowance. Pattern B should be 5½in x 7in (14cm x 17.8cm) including seam allowance.

3 For the units of the four different plum blocks, use the patterns provided to cut the pieces shown in **Fig C**. For the most economical use of the fabric, cut the patterns from width-of-fabric strips.

For Pattern A cut the fabric strips 5½in (14cm) high and place the paper pattern as shown in **Fig D**. Draw carefully around the pattern, repeating along the strip, and then cut out the shapes. You will get nine from each strip, which is more than you need. Remember that some of Pattern A will need to be reversed, so follow the shapes shown in **Fig C** carefully.

For Pattern B cut the fabric strips 7in (17.8cm) high and place the paper pattern as shown in **Fig D**. Draw, repeat and then cut out the shapes, as before. You will get eleven shapes from each strip. Remember that some shapes of Pattern B will need to be reversed.

4 For the leaf and stalk appliqués, use the patterns to cut the number of shapes given in **Fig C**. The stalk pattern includes an approximate ⅛in (3mm) seam allowance. The leaf pattern includes a ¼in (6mm) seam allowance.

5 For the top row of the quilt cut rectangles 5½in x 2½in (14cm x 6.4cm), cutting five from Fabric 25 and five from Fabric 26.

6 Cut the backing fabric in half across the width. Sew together along the long side and trim to a piece about 59in x 76in (150cm x 193cm).

7 From the binding fabric cut seven strips 2½in (6.4cm) x width of fabric. Sew together end to end and press seams open. Press in half along the length, wrong sides together.

SEWING A PLUM BLOCK

8 When all the block shapes are cut, begin to sew them together in blocks, as follows. Block 1 is described and illustrated in detail. Take the first two curved pieces (A of Fabric 1 and B of Fabric 25) and mark the halfway points along the curves by folding each piece in half and creasing or marking with a pencil (**Fig E 1**). Pin the pieces right sides together, pinning at the halfway points first (**Fig E 2**) and then at the ends. Add more pins along the curved edges, matching up the curves exactly (**Fig E 3**). Now sew the shapes together using a *scant* ¼in (6mm) seam allowance. Sew slowly and follow the curve accurately. Snip into the curved seam slightly at intervals, about ⅛in (3mm) and then press the seam to one side. Check the unit is 5½in x 7in (14cm x 17.8cm), trimming if needed (**Fig E 4**).

Fig D Cutting fabric economically

5½in (14cm)

Pattern A

7in (17.8cm)

Pattern B

Note Some A and B shapes need to be cut with these patterns rotated 180 degrees and/or reversed (flipped)

Fig E Sewing the curved shapes together

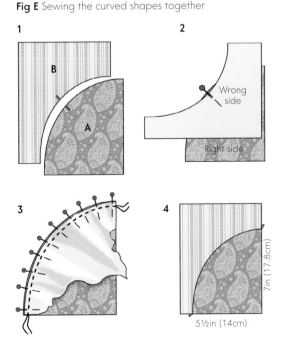

1

B

A

2

Wrong side

Right side

3

4

7in (17.8cm)

5½in (14cm)

9 Repeat this process to sew the other three curved units for Block 1, using the fabrics shown in **Fig C**. Note carefully the way the pieces are positioned.

10 To assemble the block, lay out the four units as shown in **Fig F**. Sew the units together in pairs and then sew the pairs together, matching the centre seam neatly. Check the block is 10½in x 13½in (26.7cm x 34.3cm). Using the same process, make seven of Block 1 in total.

11 Using the same process, make six each of Block 2, Block 3 and Block 4.

ASSEMBLING THE QUILT

12 For the top row of the quilt sew together the 5½in x 2½in (14cm x 6.4cm) rectangles of Fabric 25 and Fabric 26, beginning with Fabric 26 and alternating along the row. Press the seams in one direction. Check the row is 50½in (128.3cm) long.

13 Begin to sew the blocks together in rows, with five in each row, following the block order shown in **Fig G** for the first two rows and then **Fig B** for the rest of the quilt. Press the row seams in alternating directions. Once all of the rows are joined, sew them together, matching seams neatly and then press.

ADDING THE APPLIQUÉ

14 The leaf and stalk appliqués need to be added after the quilt rows are sewn together because the appliqués overlap the edges of the blocks. Make the appliqués using the patterns provided. You can trim the seam allowances down further if you wish. We used a paper piecing method, with the leaf illustrated in **Fig H**. Follow the instructions in Basic Techniques: Appliqué: Paper Piece Method. The leaf shapes have already been cut from fabric in Step 4. Make all of the leaves needed, changing fabrics as required.

15 Make the appliqué stalks using the same method. A smaller seam allowance is given on the stalk pattern. A pointed stick, such as a cocktail stick, will help you turn the edges over more easily.

16 When all of the appliqués are complete, hand sew them in position on the quilt in the positions shown in **Fig B**. Use matching thread and tiny stitches to secure them.

QUILTING AND FINISHING

17 Make a quilt sandwich of the backing fabric, wadding (batting) and quilt. Quilt as desired. Square up the quilt, trimming excess wadding and backing.

18 Use the prepared double-fold binding strip to bind your quilt (see Basic Techniques: Binding). Add a label and your quilt is finished.

Fig F Assembling a block

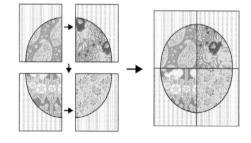

Fig H Making the appliqués

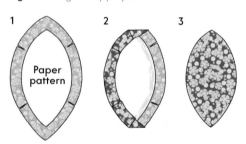

Fig G Sewing rows together

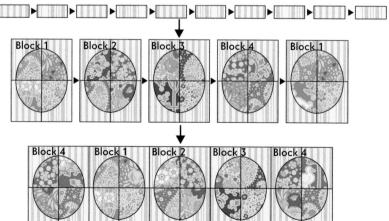

HAPPY SNOWMAN QUILT

This quilt is sure to become a classic addition to your décor at Christmas time. Rows of fun snowmen and loving hearts are displayed against a deep blue sky. The quilt is full of interest thanks to the many different colourways used for the blocks. There is also a matching pillow for the quilt – see the next chapter for the Happy Snowman Pillow.

MATERIALS

- Fabric 1: ¼yd (25cm) – Pen Stripe pink
- Fabric 2: ⅛yd (15cm) – Pen Stripe light blue
- Fabric 3: ¼yd (25cm) – Pen Stripe grey
- Fabric 4: ¼yd (25cm) – Paint Dots pink
- Fabric 5: ¼yd (25cm) – Paint Dots light blue
- Fabric 6: ¼yd (25cm) – Paint Dots grey
- Fabric 7: ¼yd (25cm) – Tiny Star pink
- Fabric 8: ⅛yd (15cm) – Tiny Star light blue
- Fabric 9: ¼yd (25cm) – Tiny Star grey
- Fabric 10: ¼yd (25cm) – Crisscross pink
- Fabric 11: ¼yd (25cm) – Crisscross light blue
- Fabric 12: ¼yd (25cm) – Crisscross grey
- Fabric 13: ¼yd (25cm) – Dottie Dots pink
- Fabric 14: ¼yd (25cm) – Dottie Dots light blue
- Fabric 15: ½yd (50cm) – Dottie Dots grey
- Fabric 16: ⅛yd (15cm) – Tiny Dots pink
- Fabric 17: ¼yd (25cm) – Tiny Dots light blue
- Fabric 18: ¼yd (25cm) – Tiny Dots grey
- Fabric 19: 2¾yd (2.5m) – Solid lupine
- Backing fabric 3½yd (3.2m)
- Wadding (batting) 61in x 79½in (155cm x 202cm)
- Binding fabric ½yd (50cm) – Pen Stripe pink
- Two packets of Tilda buttons (18 buttons) ½in (15mm) diameter (400010)
- Three packets of Tilda buttons (18 buttons) ¾in (20mm) diameter (400011)
- Black stranded embroidery cotton (floss) for embroidering eyes
- Removable fabric marker

Finished Size 52½in x 71in (133.3cm x 180.3cm)

Fig A Fabric swatches – if you can't source a fabric, replace with one in a similar colour

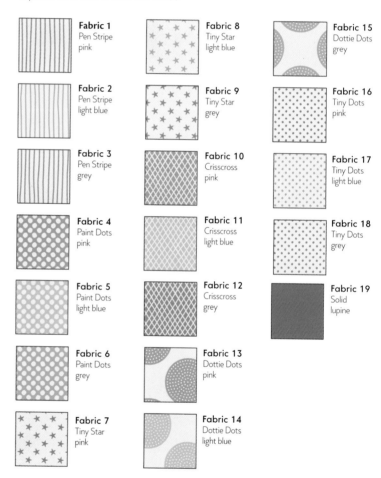

Fabric 1 Pen Stripe pink	**Fabric 8** Tiny Star light blue
Fabric 2 Pen Stripe light blue	**Fabric 9** Tiny Star grey
Fabric 3 Pen Stripe grey	**Fabric 10** Crisscross pink
Fabric 4 Paint Dots pink	**Fabric 11** Crisscross light blue
Fabric 5 Paint Dots light blue	**Fabric 12** Crisscross grey
Fabric 6 Paint Dots grey	**Fabric 13** Dottie Dots pink
Fabric 7 Tiny Star pink	**Fabric 14** Dottie Dots light blue
Fabric 15 Dottie Dots grey	
Fabric 16 Tiny Dots pink	
Fabric 17 Tiny Dots light blue	
Fabric 18 Tiny Dots grey	
Fabric 19 Solid lupine	

Fabric Note Where a long eighth or long quarter of a yard is given in the Materials list you could use fat eighths and fat quarters instead. A fat eighth is assumed to be approximately 10½in x 18in (26.7cm x 45.7cm) and a fat quarter approximately 21in x 18in (53.3cm x 45.7cm).

PREPARATION AND CUTTING OUT

1 Before you start, refer to Basic Techniques: Making Quilts and Pillows. This quilt is made up of three different blocks: a small snowman block in five different colourways, a large snowman block in a single colourway and a heart block in six different colourways. Plain horizontal sashing strips separate the quilt rows, with a pieced squares row at the top and bottom of the quilt. The fabrics used are shown in **Fig A** and the quilt layout in **Fig B**.

2 For the solid Fabric 19 long horizontal sashing strips cut these first from the *length* of the fabric, to avoid joins. Cut six strips 2in x 53in (5.1cm x 134.6cm). (You could cut the strips a little longer in case your quilt measurements differ from ours.)

3 For the solid Fabric 19 short vertical sashing strips between the heart blocks, cut from the remaining width of fabric, cutting ten strips 1⅜in x 7in (3.5cm x 17.8cm).

Fig B Quilt layout

Fig C Small snowman block layout and cutting

Small snowman top (sky)
a 8in x 2½in (20.3cm x 6.4cm).

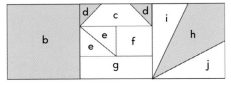

Small snowman head
b 3in (7.6cm) square.
c 3in x 1¼in (7.6cm x 3.2cm).
d 1¼in (3.2cm) square.
e 1¾in x 1½in (4.4cm x 3.8cm).
f 1¾in x 1½in (4.4cm x 3.8cm).
g 3in x 1¼in (7.6cm x 3.2cm).
h 3in (7.6cm) square.
i 1¾in x 3in (4.4cm x 7.6cm).
j 3in x 1¾in (7.6cm x 4.4cm).

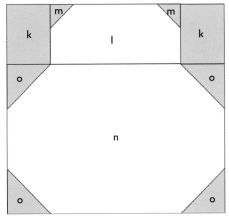

Small snowman body
k 2in x 2½in (5.1cm x 6.4cm.
l 5in x 2½in (12.7cm x 4.6cm).
m 1¼in (3.2cm) square.
n 8in x 5½in (20.3cm x 14cm).
o 2in (5.1cm) square.

4 All of the blocks use the solid Fabric 19 as a background, so there are many pieces to cut. To make things easier, you could cut these now, putting them in labelled piles. (Alternatively, you could cut them later – the pieces and their sizes are given in **Fig C**, **Fig J** and **Fig L**.) Most of the shapes are squares, so cut the fabric in strips across the width and then sub-cut into the sizes needed. The total numbers to cut for the whole quilt are given here.
- For the small snowmen – piece **a** – 8in x 2½in (20.3cm x 6.4cm). Cut 20.
- For all snowmen – piece **b** – 3in (7.6cm) square. Cut 28.
- For all snowmen – piece **d** – 1¼in (3.2cm) square. Cut 56.
- For all snowmen – piece **h** – 3in (7.6cm) square. Cut 28.
- For the small snowmen – piece **k** – 2in x 2½in (5.1cm x 6.4cm). Cut 40.
- For the large snowmen – piece **k** – 2in x 3in (5.1cm x 7.6cm). Cut 16.
- For all snowmen – piece **m** – 1¼in (3.2cm) square. Cut 56.
- For all snowmen – piece **o** – 2in (5.1cm) square. Cut 112.
- For the hearts – piece **b** – 1½in (3.8cm) square. Cut 24.
- For the hearts – piece **c** – 2in (5.1cm) square. Cut 24.
- For the hearts – piece **d** – 4½in (11.4cm) square. Cut 24.
- For the pieced squares rows – 2in (5.1cm) squares. Cut 34.

5 For the print fabrics, the exact measurements for cutting out the three different blocks are given with the block instructions and relevant diagrams. You might find it best to cut the fabrics and make the blocks one at a time, to avoid confusing all the pieces.

6 Cut the backing fabric in half across the width. Sew the pieces together along the long side. Press the seam open and trim to a piece about 61in x 79½in (155cm x 202cm).

7 From the binding fabric cut seven strips 2½in (6.4cm) x width of fabric. Sew together end to end and press the seams open. Press in half along the length, wrong sides together.

MAKING A SMALL SNOWMAN BLOCK
8 A small snowman block is made up of three sections – the top (sky), the head and the body. Each block is made the same way, but in five different colourways (Blocks A, B, C, D and E). Small snowman block A is described and illustrated in detail. **Fig C** shows the layout of the block, with the letters indicating the cut sizes of the fabric pieces. Cut out the pieces needed for one block, following exactly the measurements on the diagram. Seam allowances are included. (You may have already cut all the Fabric 19 blue solid pieces.) **Fig D** shows the different colourways for the blocks, so change fabrics depending on the colourway you are making.

9 Top (sky): This section is just a single piece of Fabric 19, cut 8in x 2½in (20.3cm x 6.4cm).

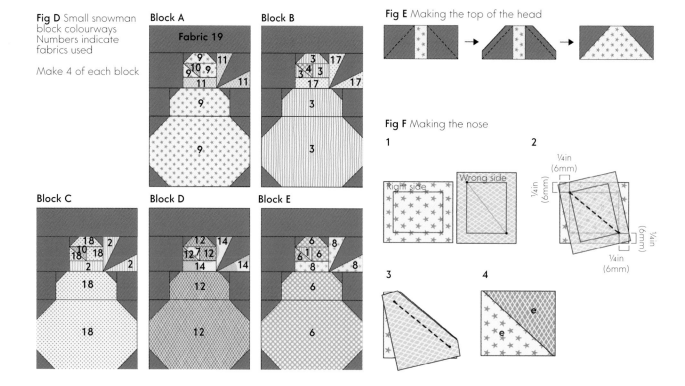

Fig D Small snowman block colourways Numbers indicate fabrics used

Make 4 of each block

Block A

Block B

Block C

Block D

Block E

Fig E *Making the top of the head*

Fig F *Making the nose*

1

2

Right side

Wrong side

¼in (6mm)

¼in (6mm)

¼in (6mm)

¼in (6mm)

3

4

e

e

10 Small snowman head: For this section you need the following pieces (see measurements **Fig C**). Block A fabrics are described here.

b – one piece of Fabric 19.

c – one piece of Fabric 9.

d – two pieces of Fabric 19.

e – one piece of Fabric 9 and one piece of Fabric 10.

f – one piece of Fabric 9.

g – one piece of Fabric 11.

h – one piece of Fabric 19.

i – one piece of Fabric 11.

j – one piece of Fabric 11.

11 Small snowman body: For this section you need the following pieces (see measurements **Fig C**).

k – two pieces of Fabric 19.

l – one piece of Fabric 9.

m – two pieces of Fabric 19.

n – one piece of Fabric 9.

o – four pieces of Fabric 19.

12 Head section: For the top of the head take a **c** piece of Fabric 9 and two **d** pieces of Fabric 19. Place the squares right sides together with the rectangle, aligning the outer edges as shown in **Fig E**. Sew along each diagonal as shown. Trim excess fabric ¼in (6mm) away from the sewn lines. Press the corner triangles outwards.

13 For the nose, take an **e** piece of Fabric 9 and using an erasable marker, mark the ¼in (6mm) seam allowance on the right side of the

fabric (**Fig F 1**). Take an **e** piece of Fabric 10 and mark the ¼in (6mm) seam allowance on the wrong side. On Fabric 10, draw a diagonal line from corner to corner of the inner shape, in the direction shown on the diagram. Place the fabrics right sides together as in **Fig F 2**, angling the pink rectangle so the ends of the diagonal line are matched with the seam allowance corners of the fabric below. Pin and then sew along the marked diagonal line (you can sew past the ends of the line). Trim excess fabric ¼in (6mm) above the sewn line (**Fig F 3**). Remove the markings and then press the seam (**Fig F 4**). Check the unit is 1¾in x 1½in (4.4cm x 3.8cm).

14 For the scarf, the angled piecing is created in a similar way to the nose. Take an **h** piece of Fabric 19 and mark the ¼in (6mm) seam allowance on the *right* side of the fabric (**Fig G 1**). Along the top edge of the square, mark a point on the marked seam allowance 1½in (3.8cm) in from the raw left-hand edge of the square, as shown. Do the same on the right-hand side of the square. Take the **i** and **j** pieces of Fabric 11 and mark the ¼in (6mm) seam allowance on the *wrong* sides. On one of the rectangles draw a diagonal line from corner to corner of the inner shape, as shown in **Fig G 1**. On the other rectangle draw the line the opposite way.

15 Place the **i** rectangle right sides together with the square, carefully aligning the lower left seam allowance points. At the top, align the end of the marked diagonal line with the 1½in (3.8cm) mark, as in **Fig G 2**. Pin in place and then sew along the marked diagonal line. Trim excess fabric ¼in (6mm) away from the sewn line (**Fig G 3**). Press the triangle outwards. Repeat this process with the other rectangle, this time angling it as shown in **Fig G 4**. Pin, sew and trim excess fabric as before, and then press (**Fig G 5**). Remove the markings and check the unit is 3in (7.6cm) square.

16 **Body section:** For the top part of the body (see **Fig H 1**), add the two **m** squares to the **l** rectangle to create corner triangles in the same way that you did for the top of the head. Now sew a piece **k** to each side of this pieced unit. For the bottom part of the body add the four **o** squares to the **n** rectangle to create corner triangles in the same way as before (**Fig H 2**). Now sew the top part of the body to the bottom part (**Fig H 3**) and press.

17 To assemble a small snowman block, follow the sequence in **Fig I**, sewing the units of the head section together first and then adding the top section and body section. Check the unfinished block is 8in x 12in (20.3cm x 30.5cm).

18 Repeat the sewing and assembly process to make twenty small snowmen blocks in total – four each of Block A, Block B, Block C, Block D and Block E (see **Fig D** for the colourways).

19 You can embroider the eye on each snowman after each block is made, or later when assembling the quilt if you prefer. Use all six strands of black embroidery cotton (floss) and French knots, winding the thread around the needle twice. See **Fig B** for the eye positions.

Fig G Making the scarf

Fig H Making the body

Fig I Assembling the small snowman block

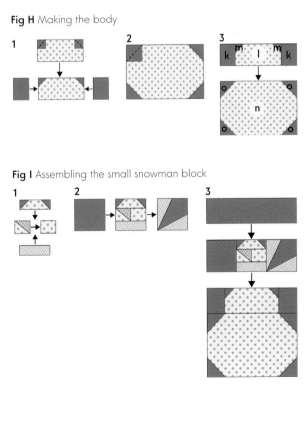

MAKING A LARGE SNOWMAN BLOCK

20 The large snowman is made in a single colourway (Block F) and doesn't have a top (sky) piece. Note that the head section is cut using the same sizes as the small snowman but in different fabrics. Follow **Fig J** for the cutting measurements and **Fig K** for the fabrics used. (You may have already cut the solid Fabric 19 pieces.)

21 Large snowman head: You need the following pieces.
b – one piece of Fabric 19.
c – one piece of Fabric 15.
d – two pieces of Fabric 19.
e – one piece of Fabric 15 and one piece of Fabric 4.
f – one piece of Fabric 15.
g – one piece of Fabric 5.
h – one piece of Fabric 19.
i – one piece of Fabric 5.
j – one piece of Fabric 5.

22 Large snowman body: You need the following pieces. Note the measurements are different from the small snowman – see **Fig J**.
k – two pieces of Fabric 19.
l – one piece of Fabric 15.
m – two pieces of Fabric 19.
n – one piece of Fabric 15.
o – four pieces of Fabric 19.

23 Large snowman head: Make the large snowman head section in the same way as the small snowman (see **Figs E, F** and **G**). Make the large snowman body section in the same way as the small snowman but using the larger pieces of fabric.

24 Assemble the large snowman in the same way as the small snowman but without the top sky piece. Check the unfinished block is 8in x 12in (20.3cm x 30.5cm). Repeat the process to make eight blocks in total.

MAKING A HEART BLOCK

25 Each heart block is made the same way, but in six different colourways (Blocks G, H, I, J, K and L). Heart block G is described and illustrated in detail. **Fig L** shows the layout of the block, with the letters indicating the cut sizes of the fabric pieces. **Fig M** shows the different colourways for the blocks, so change fabrics depending on the block you are making.

26 For a heart block you need the following pieces (see measurements in **Fig L**). Block G fabrics are described here. (You may have already cut the solid Fabric 19 pieces.)
a – two pieces of Fabric 1 (change this fabric depending on the block you are making).
b – two pieces of Fabric 19.
c – two pieces of Fabric 19.
d – two pieces of Fabric 19.

Fig J Large snowman block layout and cutting

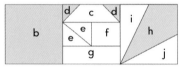

Large snowman head
Cut and sew the same as the small snowman head.

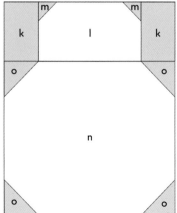

Large snowman body
k 2in x 3in (5.1cm x 7.6cm).
l 5in x 3in (12.7cm x 7.6cm).
m 1¼in (3.2cm) square.
n 8in x 7in (20.3cm x 17.8cm).
o 2in (5.1cm) square.

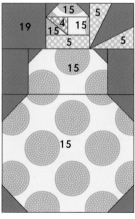

Fig K Large snowman block colourway
Numbers indicate fabrics used
Make 8 blocks

Fig L Heart block layout and cutting

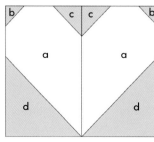

Heart
a 4½in x 7in (11.4cm x 17.8cm).
b 1½in (3.8cm) square.
c 2in (5.1cm) square.
d 4½in (11.4cm) square.

27 To make a heart block, place the print rectangle (**a**) right side up and arrange the **b**, **c** and **d** solid squares as in **Fig N 1**. Sew across the diagonals of the squares to create triangle corners. Repeat for the other side of the block, reversing the positions of the solid squares. Trim excess fabric ¼in (6mm) away from each sewn line and press the triangles outwards. Now sew the two halves of the block together (**Fig N 2**) and press. Check the unfinished block is 8½in x 7in (21.6cm x 17.8cm). Repeat to make two of each block colourway.

MAKING THE PIECED SQUARE ROWS

28 These rows are at the top and bottom of the quilt. Cut the following 2in (5.1cm) squares (this will make both rows).
• Fabric 2 – six squares.
• Fabric 5 – six squares.
• Fabric 8 – six squares.
• Fabric 11 – six squares.
• Fabric 14 – six squares.
• Fabric 17 – six squares.
• Fabric 19 – thirty-four squares (you may have already cut these).

29 Arrange the squares in sections as shown in **Fig O**. Note that there are two sections – they are identical except that Section 1 has an extra Fabric 19 square at the end. Sew the squares together using ¼in (6mm) seams and press the seams open or to one side. Repeat to make a total of four of Section 1 and two of Section 2.

30 Arrange two of Section 1 and one of Section 2 as shown in **Fig P** and then sew them together. This is the top row of the quilt. Repeat the sewing to make the bottom row.

ASSEMBLING THE QUILT

31 Follow **Fig B**, laying out the heart blocks as shown. Place a vertical sashing piece between each of the hearts. Sew all the units together using a *scant* ¼in (6mm) seam and press. A scant seam is needed so the sewn row measures 53in (134.6cm) long.

32 Following **Fig B**, lay out the snowmen blocks in the order shown. Sew each of the four rows together using normal ¼in (6mm) seams, and then press. Now lay out all of the rows of the quilt. Note that there is a long horizontal sashing strip between all of the rows of the quilt, except under the top heart row. Arrange the bottom pieced square row so it is rotated 180 degrees. Sew all the rows together and press the seams.

QUILTING AND FINISHING

33 Make a quilt sandwich of the backing fabric, wadding (batting) and quilt. Quilt as desired. Square up the quilt, trimming excess wadding and backing.

34 Use the prepared double-fold binding strip to bind your quilt (see Basic Techniques: Binding). Add a label and your quilt is finished.

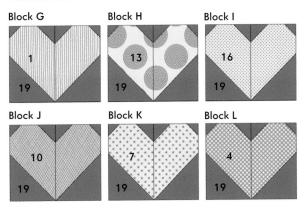

Fig M Heart block colourways
Numbers indicate fabrics used

Block G | Block H | Block I
Block J | Block K | Block L

Fig N Sewing a heart
1
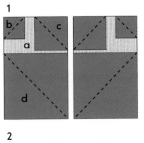

2
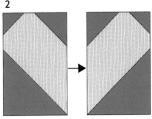

Fig O Making the pieced square rows
Numbers indicate fabrics used

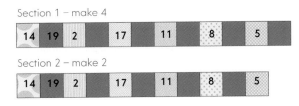

Section 1 – make 4

| 14 | 19 | 2 | | 17 | | 11 | | 8 | | 5 |

Section 2 – make 2

| 14 | 19 | 2 | | 17 | | 11 | | 8 | | 5 |

Fig P Assembling the top row

Section 1   Section 1   Section 2

Repeat the assembly for the bottom row of the quilt and then rotate it 180 degrees

HAPPY SNOWMAN PILLOW

Designed as a companion to the Happy Snowman Quilt, this comfy pillow features five of the snowman blocks from the quilt. It uses most of the same fabrics as the quilt (but not the same quantities), so refer to the fabric swatches in **Fig A** of the quilt instructions.

MATERIALS

- Fabric 2: 10in (25.4cm) square – Pen Stripe light blue
- Fabric 3: 12in (30.5cm) square – Pen Stripe grey
- Fabric 4: 5in (12.7cm) square – Paint Dots pink
- Fabric 5: 10in (25.4cm) square – Paint Dots light blue
- Fabric 7: 5in (12.7cm) square – Tiny Star pink
- Fabric 8: 5in (12.7cm) square – Tiny Star light blue
- Fabric 9: 12in (30.5cm) square – Tiny Star grey
- Fabric 10: 5in (12.7cm) square – Crisscross pink
- Fabric 11: 10in (25.4cm) square – Crisscross light blue
- Fabric 12: 12in (30.5cm) square – Crisscross grey
- Fabric 14: 10in (25.4cm) square – Dottie Dots light blue
- Fabric 15: 12in (30.5cm) square – Dottie Dots grey
- Fabric 17: 10in (25.4cm) square – Tiny Dots light blue
- Fabric 18: 12in (30.5cm) square – Tiny Dots grey
- Fabric 19: ½yd (50cm) – Solid lupine
- Wadding (batting) 42in x 22in (106.7cm x 56cm)
- Lining fabric 42in x 22in (106.7cm x 56cm) (optional)
- Fabric for pillow back, two pieces 25in x 18in (63.5cm x 45.7cm)
- Binding fabric ¼yd (25cm) – Pen Stripe pink
- Black stranded embroidery cotton (floss) for eyes
- One packet of Tilda buttons (9 buttons) ½in (15mm) diameter (400010)
- Removable fabric marker
- Pillow pad to fit cover

Finished Size 38in x 18in (96.5cm x 45.7cm)

PREPARATION AND CUTTING OUT

1 From Fabric 19 cut two sashing strips 2in x 38in (5.1cm x 96.5cm). From Fabric 19 for block backgrounds, cut the following pieces.
- For small snowmen – a – 8in x 2½in (20.3cm x 6.4cm). Cut 4.
- For all snowmen – b – 3in (7.6cm) square. Cut 5.
- For all snowmen – d – 1¼in (3.2cm) square. Cut 10.
- For all snowmen – h – 3in (7.6cm) square. Cut 5.
- For small snowman – k – 2in x 2½in (5.1cm x 6.4cm). Cut 8.
- For large snowman – k – 2in x 3in (5.1cm x 7.6cm). Cut 2.
- For all snowmen – m – 1¼in (3.2cm) square. Cut 10.
- For all snowmen – o – 2in (5.1cm) square. Cut 20.

2 From each of Fabric 2, 5, 8, 11 and 17, for the pieced squares row, cut four 2in (5.1cm) squares. From Fabric 14 cut six squares. From Fabric 19 cut twenty-four.

3 For the print fabrics, follow the measurements for cutting out the blocks in **Fig C** and **Fig J** of the quilt.

4 From binding fabric cut three strips 2½in (6.4cm) x width of fabric.

Fig A Joining the pillow rows

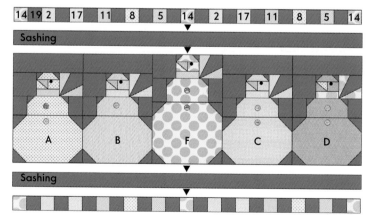

MAKING THE PATCHWORK

5 To make the small snowman follow the quilt instructions (Steps 8 to 19), making one of block A, B, C and D. To make a large snowman block F follow the quilt instructions (Steps 20 to 24). Once made, sew the snowmen together into a row, as **Fig A** here and press.

6 For a pieced squares row, lay out 2in (5.1cm) squares, alternating twelve blue with thirteen print. Sew together and press. Repeat for a second row.

7 Lay out all rows as in **Fig A** here, with a sashing strip above and below the snowman. Sew together and press.

QUILTING AND MAKING UP

8 Make a quilt sandwich and quilt as desired. Trim excess fabric. Embroider an eye on each snowman as in Step 19 of the quilt. Sew on the buttons.

9 Make up and bind the cover following the method in Basic Techniques: Bound-Edge Pillow Cover.

MATERIALS

Tilda fabrics and other materials are used predominantly for the projects in this book. The print fabrics are from various collections, including Bird Pond, Lazy Days, Plum Garden and Tea Towel Basics. We have also used some Solid fabrics and some Medium Dots fabrics. If you are not able to get hold of a fabric you can easily replace it with another fabric in a similar colour.

BACKING FABRIC

The quilts give the yardage needed for backing fabric. These amounts allow 4in (10.2cm) extra all round, to allow the quilt to be long-arm quilted. If you are quilting the project yourself then 2in (5cm) extra all round will be sufficient. The yardage given is based on the normal 42in–44in (107cm–112cm) wide fabric. If you use a wider fabric then the amount needed will need to be re-calculated. You can also sew quilting fabrics together to make a piece big enough for a patchwork backing.

WADDING (BATTING)

The wadding used is your choice and depends on the effect you want to achieve. For a normal flat and firm result, cotton wadding is recommended, especially for quilts and pillows. If you like a puffy look then a wadding with a higher loft can be used. Cut the wadding the same size as the backing.

BASIC MATERIALS AND TOOLS

The project instructions give the fabrics that are needed but you will also need some general materials and tools, including the following.
• Piecing and quilting threads.
• Rotary cutter and mat.
• Quilter's ruler – a 6½in x 24in rectangular ruler and a 12in square ruler are most useful.
• Sharp fabric scissors.
• Marking tools, such as a water-soluble pen or chalk marker.
• Thick paper or template plastic to make patterns (templates).
• Pins and hand sewing needles.

BASIC TECHNIQUES

This section describes the general techniques you will need for the projects in this book. Techniques that are specific to any individual project are given within the project instructions. Make sure you read all of the instructions before you start any of the projects and refer to the guidance below when prompted in the steps.

USING THE PATTERNS

All of the patterns for the book are given full size in the Patterns section (the next chapter). To prepare a pattern, trace or photocopy it onto thick paper (including any marks) and cut out the shape. Check the pattern is the correct, full size. Label the pattern. If a pattern is made up of two or more parts, then use adhesive tape to fix them together along the dashed lines. There are notes at the start of the Patterns section giving further guidance.

MAKING QUILTS AND PILLOWS

Follow these general guidelines when making the quilts in the book.
- Read all of the instructions through before you start.
- Fabric quantities are based on a usable width of 42in (107cm).
- Measurements are in imperial inches with metric conversions in brackets – use only *one* system throughout (preferably imperial).
- Press fabrics before cutting.
- Use ¼in (6mm) seams unless otherwise instructed.
- Press seams open or to one side, as preferred, or according to the project instructions.
- If a quilt uses a pattern (template) be sure to copy it full size. If printing it, use A4 paper size and a 100% scale.

HALF-SQUARE TRIANGLE UNITS

Many of the quilts use half-square triangle (HST) units. We describe here the common way of making these, to create two identical units.

1 Take two different fabric squares (the size given in the project instructions). Pencil mark the diagonal line on the wrong side of one of the squares (**Fig A**).

2 Pin the two squares right sides together, with all outer edges aligned. Sew ¼in (6mm) away from the marked line on each side.

3 Press the stitching and then cut the units apart on the marked line.

4 Open out each unit and press the seam (open or to one side as preferred). Check each unit is the size required.

Fig A Making half-square triangle units

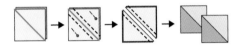

CORNER SQUARE UNIT

This method uses a square to create a triangle corner on another piece of fabric.

1 To create a corner triangle, take a small square and mark a diagonal line from corner to corner on the wrong side of the fabric (note: there is no right or wrong side on Tilda solid fabric). Place the square right side down in the corner of the base piece of fabric, with the marked line as shown in **Fig B**. Sew along the marked line and then trim off the excess corner ¼in (6mm) away from the marked line. Press the small triangle outwards.

FLYING GEESE UNIT

This method makes one unit at a time and needs one rectangle and two squares. The squares may be two different fabrics.

1 On the wrong side of the two small squares, draw or crease a diagonal line. Place a small square right side down on the rectangle (right side up), aligning the corners as shown in **Fig C**. Pin together if needed. Sew along the marked line (or a fraction outside of the line). Trim excess fabric at the back ¼in (6mm) away from the stitching line and press the triangle outwards.

2 Sew the second square to the rectangle in the same way in the opposite corner. Once sewn and pressed, this square will overlap the one already sewn in place – this will form a ¼in (6mm) seam allowance at the top of the unit.

APPLIQUÉ

Some of the projects feature appliqué and this has been achieved using two different techniques. If the shape is smooth and symmetrical the fabric can be gathered over a piece of thick card. For other shapes a paper piece technique has been used, where fabric is folded over the edges of a paper pattern and then glued and pressed into place.

GATHERING OVER CARD METHOD

1 A circle shape is illustrated here. Use the pattern (template) shape plus seam allowance to cut the shape from fabric (**Fig D 1**). Use the pattern shape minus seam allowance to cut the shape from thick card. Place this card shape in the centre of the fabric shape, on the wrong side, and use a pencil to mark the shape on the fabric (**Fig D 2**).

2 Use a doubled thread to sew a circle of gathering stitches about ⅛in (3mm) outside of the marked line (**Fig D 3**). Place the small card template back onto the fabric and pin in place. Pull up the gathering threads, to gather the fabric around the template (**Fig D 4**). Tie off the threads and press the seam well. Remove the card template and press again. You can leave the gathering thread in place if it doesn't show, or remove it.

PAPER PIECE METHOD

1 Cut out a piece of fabric using the relevant pattern – if the pattern doesn't include a seam allowance then add one approximately ⅛in (3mm) all round before cutting out.

Fig B Making a corner triangle unit

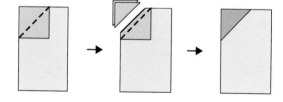

Fig D Appliqué by gathering

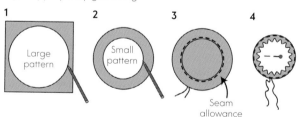

Fig C Making a flying geese unit

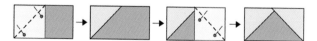

Fig E Appliqué by paper piecing

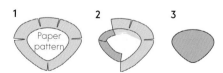

2 Snip into the seam allowance at intervals around the shape. Copy the pattern again onto paper and this time cut it out without a seam allowance. Lightly glue the pattern in the centre of the fabric shape, on the wrong side (**Fig E 1**). Smear a little fabric glue around the edges of the paper pattern and begin to fold and press the fabric edges over onto the paper, forming a smooth curve around the edge of the paper pattern (**Fig E 2**). A cocktail stick can help turn over the allowance on small pieces. Continue like this all round the shape. Remove the paper pattern and press firmly (**Fig E 3**).

QUILT SANDWICH

If you are quilting the quilt yourself you will need to make a quilt sandwich. Press the quilt top and the backing and smooth wrinkles out of the wadding (batting). Place the backing fabric right side down, place the wadding on top and then the quilt, right side up. Secure the layers of this sandwich together. This can be done in various ways, as follows.

• Use large stitches to tack (baste) a grid through the layers in both directions, with lines about 4in (10.2cm) apart.
• Use pins or safety pins to fix the layers together.
• Use fabric glue, sprayed on the wadding to fix the layers together. When the layers of the quilt are secured you can quilt as desired. If you are sending the quilt off to be commercially long-arm quilted you won't need to make a sandwich, as this is done when the quilt is mounted on the machine.

QUILTING

There are so many ways to quilt a project. The quilts in this book have been lavishly adorned with custom long-arm quilting but of course you could use much simpler patterns. For example, you could machine or hand stitch 'in the ditch' (that is, in the seams) of each block. Another easy method is to follow the shapes of the block, quilting about ¼in (6mm) away from the seams. If you prefer not to quilt yourself then you could send the quilt off to a long-arm quilter, who will do all the work for you.

BINDING

The binding used for the projects in the book is a double-fold binding, using strips cut 2½in (6.4cm) wide x width of fabric. You can sew the binding strips together using straight seams, or diagonal (45-degree) seams if you prefer.

1 When all of the binding strips have been joined together, press the binding in half all along the length, wrong sides together.

2 Follow **Fig F**. Sew the binding to the quilt sandwich by pinning the raw edge of the folded binding against the raw edge of the quilt front. Don't start at a corner. Using a ¼in (6mm) seam, sew the binding in place, starting at least 6in (15.2cm) away from the end of the binding. Sew to within a ¼in (6mm) of a corner and stop. Take the quilt off the machine and fold the binding upwards, creating a

Fig F Binding

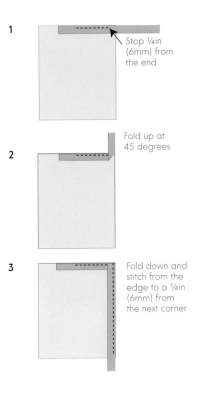

1   Stop ¼in (6mm) from the end

2   Fold up at 45 degrees

3   Fold down and stitch from the edge to a ¼in (6mm) from the next corner

45-degree angle. Hold this in place, fold the binding back down and pin it in place. Begin sewing the ¼in (6mm) seam again from the top of the folded binding to within ¼in (6mm) of the next corner and then repeat the mitring process. Do this on all corners. Leave about 6in (15.2cm) of unsewn binding at the end.

3 To join the two ends of the binding, open up the beginning and end of the binding tails, lay them flat and fold the ends back so the two folded ends touch. Mark these folds by creasing or with pins – this is where your seam needs to be. Open out the binding and sew the pieces together at these creases with a straight seam. Trim off excess fabric and press the seam. Re-fold the binding in half and finish stitching it in place on the front of the quilt.

4 With the quilt right side up, use a medium-hot iron to press the binding outwards all round. Now begin to turn the binding over to the back of the quilt, pinning it in place. Use matching sewing thread and slipstitch the binding in place all round, creating neat mitres at each corner. Press the binding and your quilt is finished.

BOUND-EDGE PILLOW COVER

All of the pillows in the book are made up with a bound edge, using prepared double-fold binding.

1 To make up the pillow cover, on both pieces of fabric for the pillow back, create a hem along one long side of each piece, by turning the edge over by about ½in (1.3cm), twice. Sew the seam with matching thread and press (**Fig G 1**).

2 The pieces for the pillow are assembled with right sides out, as follows. Place the quilted patchwork right side down. Pin one backing piece on top, right side up and with the hem towards the centre. Pin the second backing piece on top, right side up and hem towards the centre (so the backing pieces overlap). Make sure the outer edges of all three pieces are aligned (**Fig G 2**). Pin the layers together and then bind as normal. As you sew the binding in place it will fix the other layers together, although you could tack (baste) them first if you prefer. Press the cover and insert a pillow pad to finish.

Fig G Bound-edge pillow cover

1

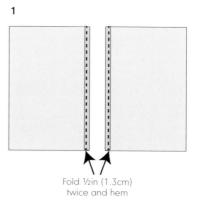

Fold ½in (1.3cm) twice and hem

2

PATTERNS

- All of the patterns are given full size.
- Some have been split up to fit on the page. Thick dashed lines show where two parts of a pattern have to be joined, shown by A and B points, which need to be matched.
- In most cases, the patterns include seam allowances. If not, refer to the advice with the specific patterns.

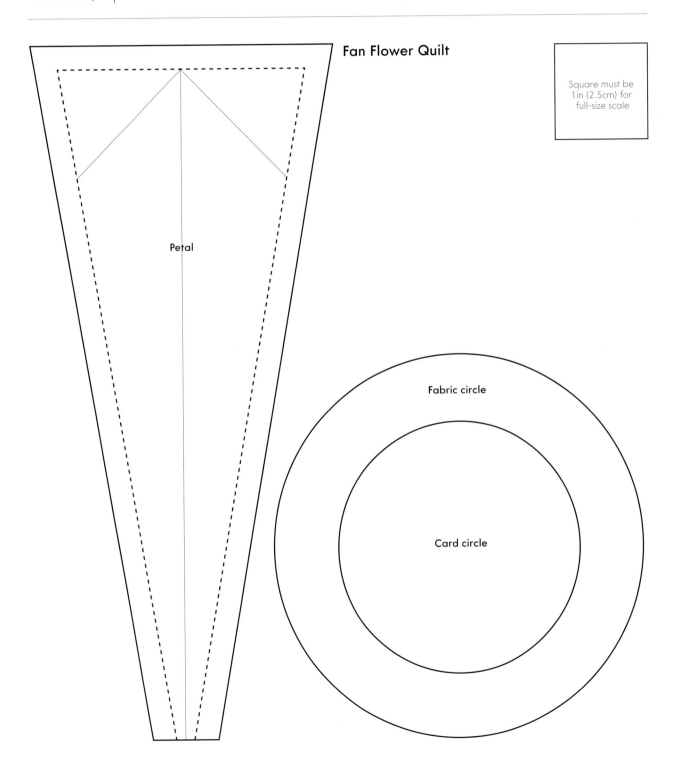

Fan Flower Quilt

Square must be 1in (2.5cm) for full-size scale

Petal

Fabric circle

Card circle

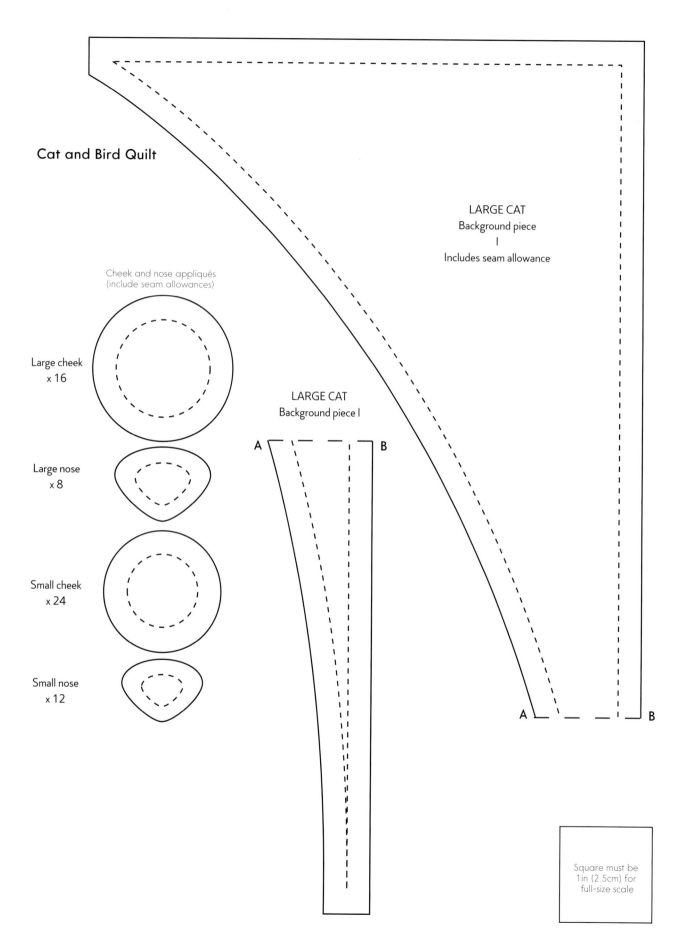

Cat and Bird Quilt

Cheek and nose appliqués
(include seam allowances)

Large cheek
x 16

Large nose
x 8

Small cheek
x 24

Small nose
x 12

LARGE CAT
Background piece
I
Includes seam allowance

LARGE CAT
Background piece I

A   B

A   B

Square must be
1in (2.5cm) for
full-size scale

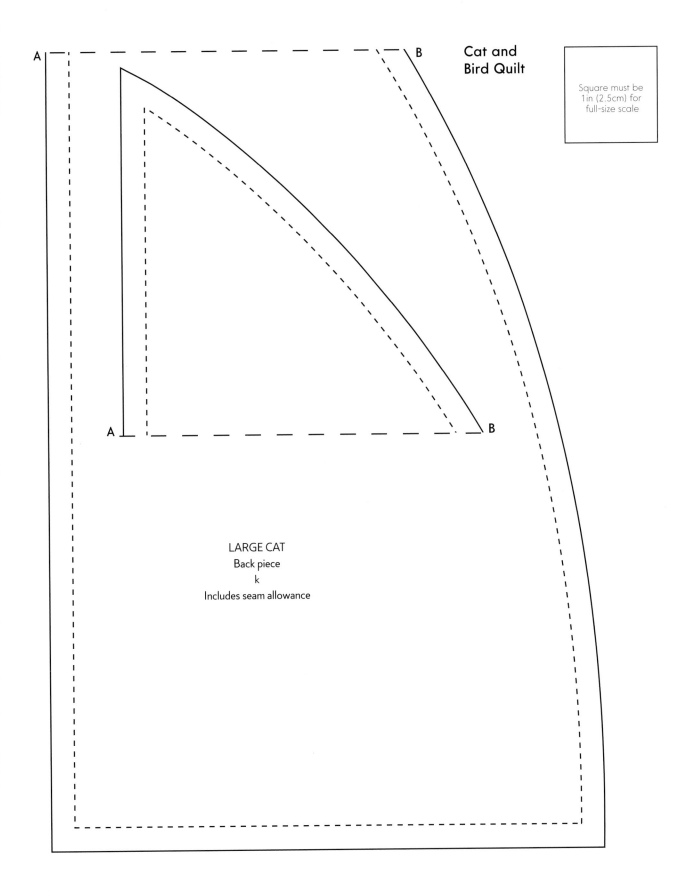

Cat and
Bird Quilt

Square must be
1in (2.5cm) for
full-size scale

LARGE CAT
Back piece
k
Includes seam allowance

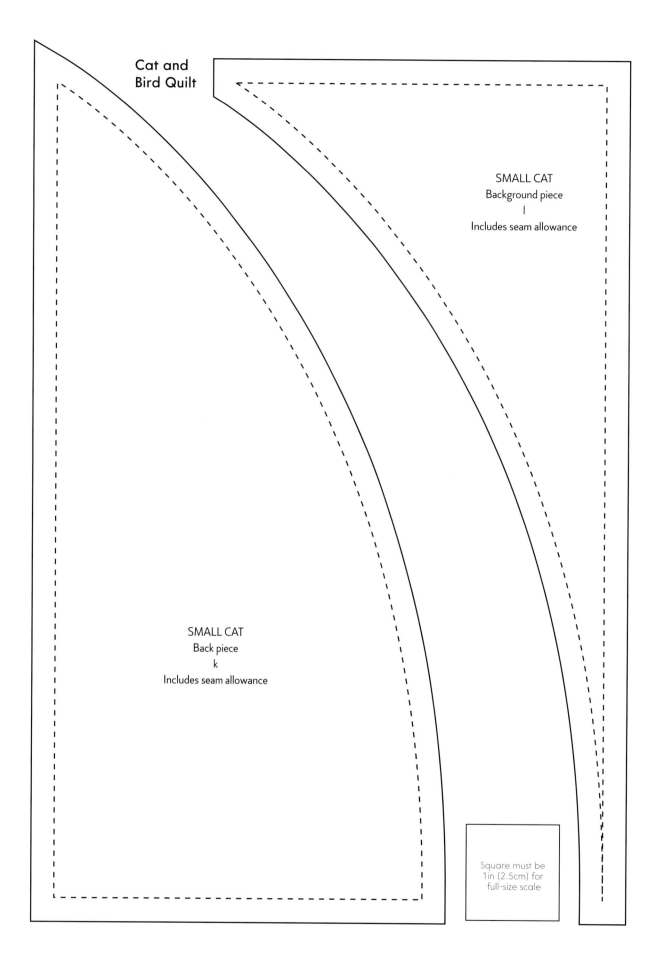

Cat and
Bird Quilt

SMALL CAT
Background piece
l
Includes seam allowance

SMALL CAT
Back piece
k
Includes seam allowance

Square must be
1in (2.5cm) for
full-size scale

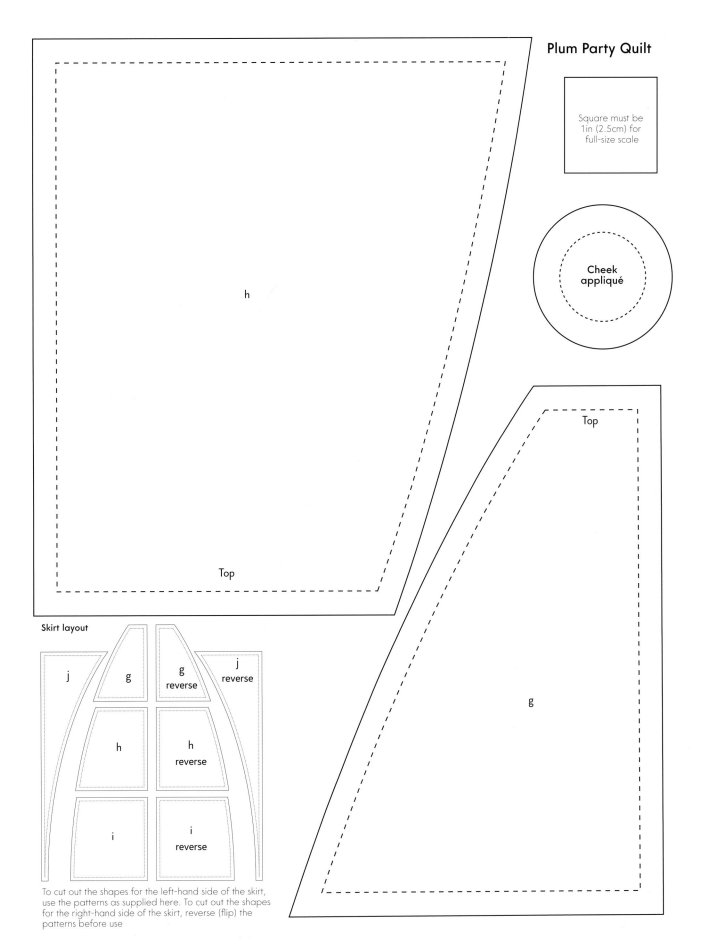

Plum Party Quilt

Square must be 1in (2.5cm) for full-size scale

Cheek appliqué

h

Top

Top

g

Skirt layout

j | g | g | j
 | | reverse | reverse

h | h
 | reverse

i | i
 | reverse

To cut out the shapes for the left-hand side of the skirt, use the patterns as supplied here. To cut out the shapes for the right-hand side of the skirt, reverse (flip) the patterns before use

Plum Party Quilt

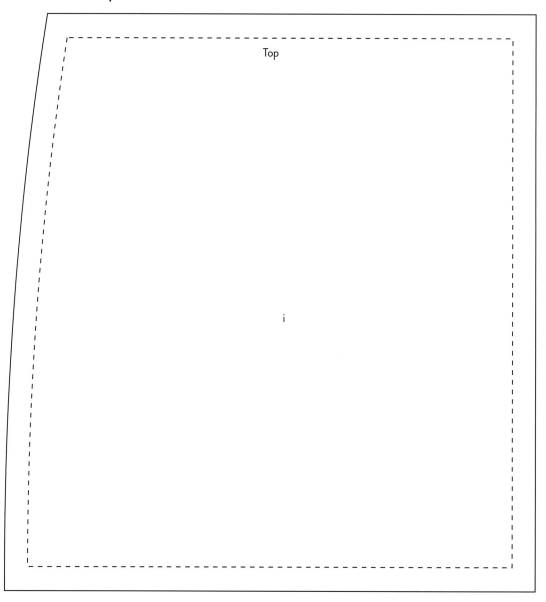

Top

i

Square must be
1in (2.5cm) for
full-size scale

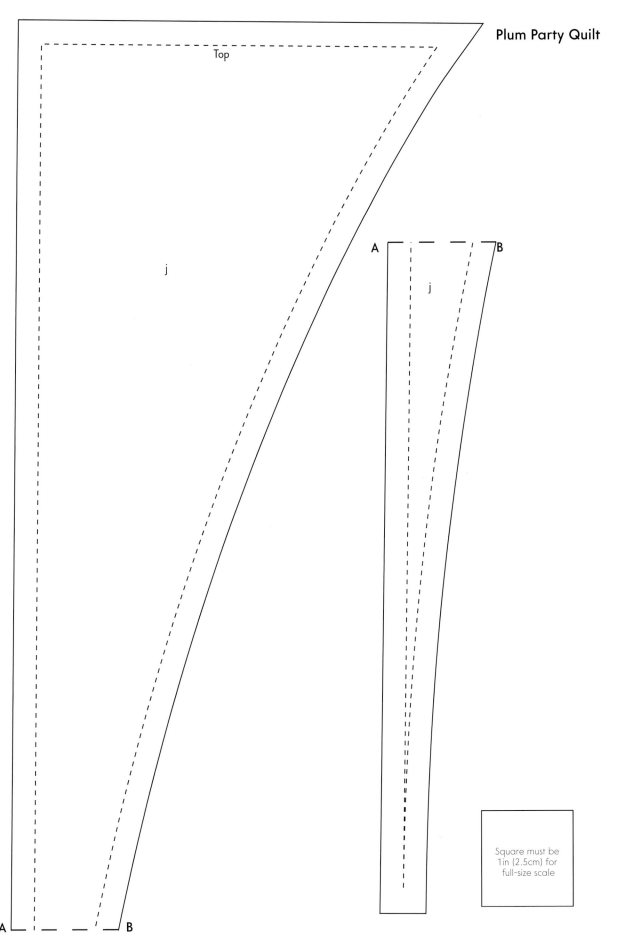

Plum Party Quilt

Top

j

A   B

A   B

j

Square must be
1in (2.5cm) for
full-size scale

A   B

Plum Quilt

Use the full-size patterns for each block, rotating and reversing the shapes as indicated in this diagram

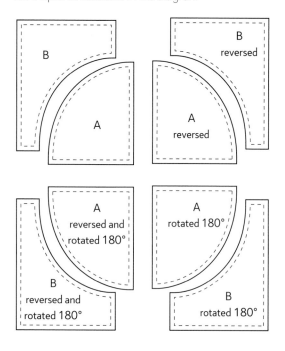

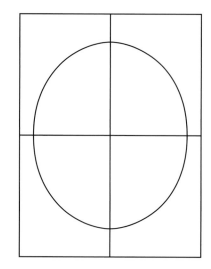

Plum Garden Village Quilt

Bee appliqué patterns

Before cutting out fabric add an approximate ⅛in (3mm) seam allowance all round

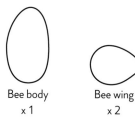

Bee body
x 1

Bee wing
x 2

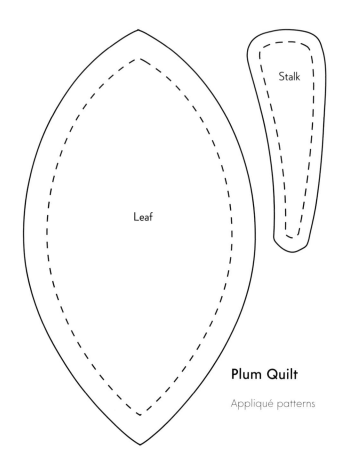

Leaf

Stalk

Plum Quilt

Appliqué patterns

Square must be
1in (2.5cm) for
full-size scale

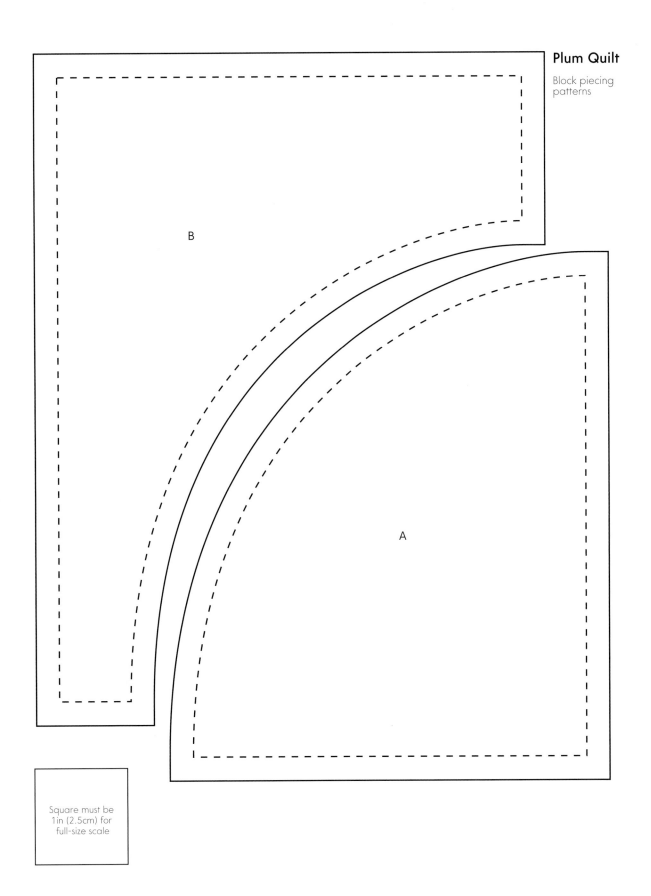

Plum Quilt

Block piecing patterns

B

A

Square must be 1in (2.5cm) for full-size scale

SUPPLIERS

Tilda fabric is stocked in many stores worldwide. To find your nearest Tilda retailer, please search online or contact the Tilda wholesaler in your territory. For more information visit www.tildafabrics.com.

EUROPE

Marienhoffgarden
Germany, Holland, Belgium, Austria, Luxembourg, Switzerland and Denmark
Industrivej 39
DK 8550 Ryomgaard
Denmark
Phone: +45 86 39 55 15
Email: mail@marienhoff.dk
www.marienhoff.dk

Industrial Textiles
Sweden, Norway and Germany
Engholm Parkvej 1
3450 Allerød
Denmark
Phone: +45 48 17 20 55
Email: mail@indutex.dk
www.indutex.dk

Groves
UK
Eastern Bypass Thame
Oxfordshire, OX9 3FU UK
Phone: +44 (0) 1844 258 080
Email: sales@groves-banks.com
www.grovesltd.co.uk

Rhinetex
France, Germany, Benelux
Maagdenburgstraat 24
7421 ZC Deventer
The Netherlands
Phone: +31 (0)570 2345 26
E-mail: info@rhinetex.com
https://rhinetex.com

Bordelay S.L.
Spain and Portugal
C/Atlantico, 6
Pol. Ind. Los Olivos
28864 Ajalvir
Madrid
Phone: +34 91.887.40.41
www.bordelay.com

J. Pujol Maq Conf S.A.
Spain and Portugal
Pol. Ind. Les Pedreres, sector B
C/ Industria n°5
08390 Montgat
BARCELONA (Spain)
Phone: + 34 933 511 611
Email: jmpairo@jpujol.com
www.ideaspatch.com

Fátima Cadima
Portugal
Largo António Joaquim Correia, 4A
2900-231 Setúbal
Phone: +351 265 573 656
Email: mail@indutex.dk
www.fatimacadima.com.pt
Email: manualidadesfc@iol.pt

STIM Italia Srl
Italy
Viale Carlo Troya 7
20144 MILANO
Italy
Phone: +39 02 8423 0628
Mobile: +39 392 923 6898
Email: info@stim-italia.com
www.stim-italia.com
Instagram: tilda_italia

Marčik Látky
Czech Republic
Hradební 1235
686 01 Uherské Hradiště
Phone.: +420 775 195 550
Email: info@marciklatky.cz
www.marciklatky.cz

NORTH AMERICA

Brewer Quilting & Sewing Supplies
USA and South America
3702 Prairie Lake Court,
Aurora, I L 60504, US
Phone: + 1 630 820 5695
Email: info@brewersewing.com
www.brewersewing.com

JN Harper
Canada, North America
8335 Devonshire Rd.
Montreal, Quebec
H4P 2L1
Canada
Phone: +1 514 736 3000
Email: info@jnharper.com
www.jnharper.com

AUSTRALIA

Two Green Zebras
Australia, New Zealand
Po Box 530 Tewantin
Queensland 4565
Phone: +61 (0) 2 9553 7201
Email: sales@twogreenzebras.com
www.twogreenzebras.com
Instagram: tilda_australia

AFRICA

Barrosa Trading Trust (Liefielove)
South Africa
Kogel Street 9D Middelburg
Mpumalanga ,1050
South Africa
Phone: +27 (0) 847 575 177
Email: liefielove11@gmail.com
www.liefielove.co.za

ASIA

Sing Mui Heng Ltd,
Singapore
315 Outram Road, #05-09
Tan Boon Liat Building
Singapore 169074
Phone: +65 6221 9209
Email: enquiry@singmuiheng.com
www.smhcraft.com

M&S Solution
South Korea
Gangnam B/D 7F, 217, Dosan-daero,
Gangnamww-gu, Seoul,
South Korea
Phone: +82 (2) 3446 7650
Email: godsky0001@gmail.com

Scanjap Incorporated
Japan, Hong Kong and Indonesia
Chiyoda-ku, Kudan-minami 3-7-12
Kudan Tamagawa Bld. 3F
102-0074 Tokyo, Japan
Phone: +81 3 6272 9451
Email: info@scanjap.com
www.tildajapan.com
Instagram: tildajapantokyo

Long Teh Trading Co. Ltd.
Taiwan
No. 71, Hebei W. St.
Beitun Dist. Taichung City 40669
Taiwan
Phone: +886 4 2247 7711
Email: longteh.quilt@gmail.com
www.patchworklife.com.tw/index.asp

Quilt Friends
Malaysia
C-G-33, G/Floor Block Camilia,
10 Boulevard, Sprint Highway,
Kayu Ara PJU6A, 47400 Petaling Jaya,
Selangor D.E
Malaysia
Phone: +60 377 293 110
Email: quilt_friends@outlook.com
www.quiltfriends.net

Mianhexin Trading Co.,Ltd. (FlowerQuilt)
China
Room 1001, New World Serviced
Apartment, NO.136
West Taige Road, Yixing City,
Jiangsu Province, 214200
Phone: + 86 (510) 8792 6550
Email: flowerquilt@hotmail.com
www.flowerquilt.cn

T.G.H International Ltd.
Thailand
55/5-6 Soi Phaholyothin 11
Phaholythin Rd., Samsennai
Phayathai,
10400 Bangkok, Thailand
Email: tghinter@truemail.co.th